Structural changes are having profound impacts on the telecommunications sector in OECD countries. These changes arise from economic, institutional and technological factors. This report reviews structural change in telecommunications in those countries. It was undertaken by Mr. Dimitri Ypsilanti of the division of Information, Computer and Communications Policies in the OECD's Directorate for Science, Technology and Industry, as a contribution to the OECD's overall study on structural adjustment. The report was submitted to the Committee on Information, Computer and Communications Policies and to the Industry Committee, which recommended that it be made available to the public on the responsibility of the Secretary-General who subsequently agreed.

Also available

ICCP "INFORMATION, COMPUTER AND COMMUNICATIONS POLICY" Series

No. 13 – TRENDS OF CHANGE IN TELECOMMUNICATIONS POLICY (April 1987)
(93 87 02 1) ISBN 92-64-12940-5   354 pages   £12.50   US$25.00   F125.00   DM56.00

No. 12 – INFORMATION TECHNOLOGY AND ECONOMIC PROSPECTS (April 1987)
(93 87 01 1) ISBN 92-64-12927-8   222 pages   £9.50   US$19.00   F95.00   DM42.00

No. 11 – TRENDS IN THE INFORMATION ECONOMY (September 1986)
(93 86 03 1) ISBN 92-64-12861-1   42 pages   £4.00   US$8.00   F40.00   DM19.00

No. 10 – COMPUTER-RELATED CRIME: ANALYSIS OF LEGAL POLICY (August 1986)
(93 86 01 1) ISBN 92-64-12852-2   72 pages   £4.00   US$8.00   F40.00   DM20.00

No. 9 – SOFTWARE: AN EMERGING INDUSTRY (September 1985)
(93 85 04 1) ISBN 92-64-12755-0   204 pages   £12.00   US$24.00   F120.00   DM53.00

No. 8 – AN EXPLORATION OF LEGAL ISSUES IN INFORMATION AND COM-MUNICATION TECHNOLOGIES (January 1984)
(93 83 03 1) ISBN 92-64-12527-2   136 pages   £7.00   US$14.00   F70.00   DM31.00

No. 7 – MICRO-ELECTRONICS, ROBOTICS AND JOBS (May 1983)
(93 82 02 1) ISBN 92-64-12384-9   266 pages   £12.50   US$25.00   F125.00   DM62.00

VENTURE CAPITAL IN INFORMATION TECHNOLOGY (March 1985)
(93 85 02 1) ISBN 92-64-12696-1   54 pages   £5.50   US$11.00   F55.00   DM25.00

TELECOMMUNICATIONS. Pressures and Policies for Change (April 1983)
(93 83 02 1) ISBN 92-64-12428-4   142 pages   £6.90   US$14.00   F69.00   DM34.00

GUIDELINES ON THE PROTECTION OF PRIVACY AND TRANSBORDER FLOWS OF PERSONAL DATA (February 1981)
(93 81 01 1) ISBN 92-64-12155-2   42 pages   £3.00   US$6.00   F30.00   DM13.00

To be Published

ICCP "INFORMATION, COMPUTER AND COMMUNICATIONS POLICY" Series

No. 15 – SATELLITES AND FIBER OPTICS: Competition and Complementarity

No. 16 – NEW TELECOMMUNICATION SERVICES: Videotex Development Strategies.

Prices charged at the OECD Bookshop.

THE OECD CATALOGUE OF PUBLICATIONS and supplements will be sent free of charge on request addressed either to OECD Publications Service, 2, rue André-Pascal, 75775 PARIS CEDEX 16, or to the OECD Distributor in your country.

Published by North-Holland Publishing Co., Netherlands on behalf of the OECD:

CHANGING MARKET STRUCTURES IN TELECOMMUNICATIONS
ISBN 0-444-85327-3   276 pages   US$67.50   DFL.180.00

TRANSBORDER DATA FLOWS – PROCEEDINGS OF AN OECD CONFERENCE
ISBN 0-444-87700-2   US$74.00   DFL.200.00

Both publications available from:
    Elsevier Science Publishers,
    P.O. Box 211
    1000 A E Amsterdam
    The Netherlands

and in the USA and Canada from:
    Elsevier Science Publishing Inc.,
    P.O. Box 1663
    Grand Central Station,
    New York, N.Y. 10163
    United States

TABLE OF CONTENTS

SUMMARY

The aim of this study is to describe briefly the challenges arising from structural change in telecommunications. These are moving to the forefront of domestic and international economic policy debates in view of the important role telecommunications networks are beginning to play in the advanced economies. As the information age sweeps over OECD economies there will be an increasing need to allow for unconstrained growth and development of telecommunications-intensive manufacturing and service industries.

Economic analysis has not traditionally applied the concept of structural adjustment to growth industries. However, factors which impede growth can lead to longer-term structural problems. In particular, policies which maintain capital and labour resources in declining sectors may impede the transfer of resources to growth sectors. Similarly, impediments on growth sectors may be policy-induced or can be removed through effective policies. Such policies may at a time when under- or unutilised resources exist elsewhere within the economy, also constrain adjustment in other sectors. At the international level, resource misallocation can be trade-distorting and lead to international structural adjustment problems and to international economic frictions. It is in this context that the telecommunications industry has been chosen for examination.

Since the 1970s there has been a range of developments driven by the increasing information requirements of large business users and governments, the use of information in controlling costs and the importance of information as a factor in improving competitiveness. These developments, which have shown a marked acceleration in the 1980s, have been facilitated by structural change, and have influenced the economic and institutional structure of telecommunications. The telecommunications service industry, which was historically considered as a utility – much like the electric power industry – providing a universal service and requiring a high degree of regulation and central administration, is now considered an important factor in the growth of the manufacturing and service sectors and in competitiveness. Reference needs to be made, in particular, to the increasing role of services and information in the economies of OECD countries and to rapid technological change in telecommunications equipment (switching, transmission and terminal equipment) and in particular the merging of computer and communications technology. Both these factors have enhanced the role of communications in economic activity and have led to a proliferation of new telecommunications services or enhanced the quality and capability of existing services.

Telecommunications has helped increase productivity, improve cost performance and provide the means for the generation of new service and manufacturing activities. Already telecommunications is having significant positive spillover effects on other sectors, such as banking, financial markets, tourism, and other information and computer service industries. Structural problems in telecommunications, which constrain the growth and diffusion of the industry's services, can have far-reaching economy-wide repercussions which may become crucial in future years. It is therefore necessary that policy formulation in telecommunications is widened to include general economic and trade policy.

Three aspects of telecommunications need to be addressed. First, adjustment in services, its impact and lessons. Second, adjustment in the equipment industry, the impact and the lessons learned from this process. Third, adjustment in telecommunications and its economy-wide and sectoral impact. Each of these aspects contain a wide range of issues requiring complicated and lengthy analysis to which the present study can only do partial justice, and only on a selective basis. Many new issues will also arise both as technology and institutional frameworks change.

This study begins by examining the role of telecommunications in the economy. The telecommunications service industry has, in most OECD countries, grown at a higher rate than Gross Domestic Product, and telecommunications investment has been important in the growth of gross fixed capital formation. It is clear that the telecommunications industry provides the backbone supporting a wide range of growing service industries, and has the potential to create many new service activities. Similarly, obvious trends in intra-firm, inter-firm and intersectoral networking structures attest to the growing strategic importance of telecommunications. The dynamism of the communications industry is also an important factor in stimulating innovation and research and development in a range of related sectors.

The examination of structural characteristics and change in telecommunications services (Chapter II) shows that despite significant growth in networks, many telecommunications administrations have been extremely slow in meeting the requirements of universal service: only in recent years has there been an accelerated effort to this end. An examination of relative operating performances of common carriers indicates a wide dispersion of results unrelated to size of carriers. The extent to which scale itself is an important factor in cost saving for network operators needs to be further examined. The requirement to augment revenue growth, however, is becoming an important factor for telephone administrations, which have usually taken one of two general approaches. The first has been to allow free rein to the market to stimulate new communications-based services while the second has been to extend the mandate of the telecommunications administrations by providing common-carrier controlled services. It must be understood, as argued in Chapter III, that existing telecommunications structures are no longer adequate, and that reference can no longer be made to static concepts to justify existing policies. Nevertheless, it must be recognised that there can be diversity of solutions to realise telecommunications goals. The issue of competition in telecommunications services is closely tied to questions of tariffication and costing procedures. At the same time, it must be recognised that equity and neutrality conditions imply a need for change in the regulatory and policy formulation structures in many countries.

In the telecommunications equipment industry structural changes have been occurring over the last decade, as shown in Chapter IV, and present trends indicate that some significant adjustment in the industry's structure is likely to continue. In particular, while parts of the industry have been characterised by growth in the number of firms and diversification, the major part of the industry producing central office switching equipment is consolidating and contracting in terms of number of firms, and intensifying competition at the same time.

The similarity in international telecommunications structures has fragmented as a result of diverging trends in the adjustment of service structures. There is therefore an urgent need for a new international consensus in telecommunications policy which takes into account the reality of technological change and which allows consumers, manufacturing and service industries to benefit fully from the potential which is offered by new communications services

7

and technologies, particularly in transforming their own production structures. The challenge of structural change in telecommunications is to meet the diverging needs of service users and balance the social goals of providing universal service with economic goals of efficient telecommunications services responding to the requirements of manufacturing and service industries.

The fast rate of change in the telecommunications industry affecting regulatory and market structures, technologies, equipment and services often imply that studies such as this can be overtaken by events. The present study, which was completed in June 1987, reflects as much as possible the situation existing at that time.

Chapter I

INTRODUCTION

Major structural changes have affected the telecommunications industry during the past decade. These changes have encompassed technology, regulatory frameworks, market structures, and industry output and have transformed the industry's image from that of a placid public utility offering a limited service and operating in an unchanging market structure, to an industry at the forefront of technological change, providing a range of services and products and destined to transform societies and economic structures. Present technological trends indicate that telecommunications will affect and become pervasive in all aspects of social and economic relations.

Only a few OECD countries have taken drastic steps to alter telecommunications structures; other countries have been more cautious taking measured steps to change their structures, while still others have deliberately avoided or delayed change. It is, however, noteworthy that a number of OECD countries have reviewed or are in the process of reviewing their telecommunications policy. At the international level differences in the rate of change in market and regulatory structures have been a prime factor in placing telecommunications questions in the forefront of international economic discussions.

1. Description of the Sector

The telecommunications sector, broadly defined, is both a service activity and a manufacturing industry. Telecommunications, which is limited in the present study to point-to-point communications (voice, data, record) – and therefore excludes broadcasting – includes:

- The production of equipment (switching, transmission, and terminal equipment) which interconnect to provide the infrastructure and networks for telecommunications services;
- The infrastructure for the provision of universal telecommunications services on a national and international basis (voice, telex, telegraphy);
- The networks and equipment for enhanced telecommunications services (voice, data, video, and facsimile) which are based on the convergence of computer and telecommunications technology and which are forming the basis for a wide range of new industries.

Approximately one-third of the telecommunications industry's activities can be accounted for by equipment production and the remaining two-thirds derive from service revenues.

Historically, the provision of telecommunications services has been highly regulated in all OECD countries. The development of the regulatory, legal and operational framework has been such as to tie closely together the service and equipment sides of the industry. This interlocking relationship, now in the process of change, has been important in nearly all countries with an equipment industry.

9

Two factors have been important in changing telecommunications and therefore in the description of the sector. Firstly, supply has changed from simply building up the network, i.e. fulfilling the goal of universal service and automated long-distance dialling, to advancing the quality of the network and meeting diversified telecommunications service needs particularly from business customers. Secondly, demand characteristics have changed, especially in the business market which now views information activities and, therefore, communications (voice, data and document interchange) as a necessary and important factor in day-to-day activities. The need to respond to those changes linked with the rapid advancement of technological innovation have created pressures for reform in telecommunications legislation and administrative structures throughout the OECD. Responses to these pressures have however, varied, reflecting in part philosophical arguments, in part differences in national market characteristics, and to a large extent the differences in the market structure – that is, whether telecommunications services were offered by state monopolies or privately regulated companies.

It is necessary to recognise that the telecommunications industry (equipment and services) includes many products and services each with distinct markets, demand characteristics and changing supply characteristics. The sections below briefly describe some of these markets.

i) Telecommunications Equipment

The complexity of the communications market makes it difficult to obtain exact and comparable data for different countries. Often data cover communications broadly defined, which includes radio and television broadcasting, radar, search and detection equipment, and telephone and telegraph equipment. Even the distinction sometimes made between "wired" communications equipment and "wireless" equipment is not helpful since the latter also includes equipment used for point-to-point communications.

Three main branches of the equipment industry can be identified:

- *Transmission equipment* (e.g. equipment for carrier systems, line apparatus for long-distance communications, radio relay equipment, microwave systems, apparatus for signal conditioning of satellites): that is equipment which functions to forward information. Cables and wire (including fibre-optics) can be included under this heading or as a separate branch;
- *Switching equipment* (e.g. exchanges, other switching equipment, switchboards, packet mode switching and circuit switched data network equipment);
- *Customer premises equipment* (e.g. telephone handsets, key systems, private branch exchanges, data terminals) which is sometimes referred to as terminal equipment.

It is difficult to generalise as to which branch is the most important for the OECD area as a whole. In the United States customer premises equipment accounts for about two-fifths of sales as a result of liberalised attachment regulations, whereas in other countries such equipment sales are less important. On the other hand, data on world sales of equipment indicate a much more even distribution between the three branches. Present developments in transmission technology (e.g. fibre-optics) and in switching equipment (conversion to digital switches) will stimulate these two branches, while the diffusion of information technology in manufacturing and service industry, will stimulate customer premises equipment. On the other hand some product areas are perceived as reaching saturation (telephone sets) or slow growth (PBXs).

ii) Telecommunications Services

The definition and description of the telecommunications services market is complicated by changing service availabilities and changing national definitions. Often a breakdown between basic and enhanced/value-added services is proposed. In such a breakdown, basic services include voice transmission, telegraphy, telex, and all other services are included under the enhanced label. But there is little agreement, often even at the national level, as to what constitutes a network function or can be considered as a service function. Technological change and evolving service concepts will also influence boundaries between services which may be considered value-added at present and basic in the future. The lack of internationally accepted definitions as to how services should be classified is also becoming of increasing concern. Because of the lack of definitions, the neat classification of services as shown in the table below is useful only as a general indicator of the possible evolution in the range of potential services which may emerge:

Three generations of telecommunications services

Present services	New services	Possible future services
Telephony	Digitized telephony	Videotelephony
Telex, teletex	Textfax	Fast facsimile
Low-speed data	Videoconferencing	Bulk document transfer
Mobile telephony	Audiographic teleconferencing	High-speed data
Low-speed facsimile	Electronic mail	High quality videotex
	Wider availability of mobile telephony	On-line graphic design
		Remote printing and publishing
	Higher resolution videotex	Dynamic computer load-sharing
		Burst-mode host-to-host transfer

Source: Based on Malcolm Ross, "Investment Opportunities in Telecommunications Markets in Europe", paper presented to the 1985 Symposium of the European Venture Capital Association, Amsterdam.

This breakdown of services provides some flavour of the actual and expected evolution in the service framework. But the table also immediately indicates a key policy problem in telecommunications – the wide range of new services with their revenue potential, attracting potential private suppliers, as well as existing network operators, and the potential inter-service competition which could erode revenue bases. It should be stressed that the range of services which add value to basic transmission on the telecommunications network or telecommunications based information services is wide. For some of these services the value-added, relative to transmission costs is low (e.g. protocol conversion), for others there is a much higher value-added (such as for inventory control based on networks).

Services may be offered on public switched telephone networks (PSTN), public switched data networks (PSDN), on private telecommunications networks and through leased lines. It is clear from the emerging potential range of services that telecommunications services can no longer be viewed as being only a delivery service concerned with the transfer of information, but are increasingly interlinked with the generation, storage, processing, and distribution of information.

2. Role of Telecommunications in OECD Countries

Macroeconomic role

The OECD area accounts for 79 per cent of the present world stock of telephone sets[1] and 78 per cent of world main lines[2] even though population represents some 17 per cent of the world total[3]. Evidently OECD has a major role in worldwide telecommunications both in terms of its market dominance but also in terms of a supplier of services, equipment and in terms of technology.

This section highlights some of the main economic indicators in order to assess the role of telecommunications in OECD economies. Although the importance of telecommunications is evident from the data, they underestimate this importance, especially given the difficulty in evaluating private sector telecommunications-related investments and activity[4]. Analysis, which has been undertaken on the contribution of telecommunications to economic growth, concludes that the role of telecommunications is substantial, especially in countries and regions with lower incomes[5]. Little analytical work is available to show the contribution of telecommunications to economic growth in the industrialised countries and how or whether this role is changing.

Four variables are examined in order to place in perspective the role of telecommunications in OECD economies: telecommunications service income, investment, exports, and production. In the present context these variables are only provided in terms of ratios to gross domestic product or total manufacturing trade. The growth and development of these variables is examined in Chapters II and III.

Total income from telecommunications services as a percentage of gross domestic product has been growing in all OECD countries, in some cases with a significant rate of growth (Table 1*). This income reached a level of $199 billion in 1985 for the OECD in total. As expected, countries with a relatively underdeveloped telecommunications network in the 1970s show high growth in service revenue (e.g. Portugal, Turkey, Ireland, France) as a result of the rapid build-up of this network.

The importance of such income in GDP depends not only on the development of the telecommunications infrastructure and diffusion of equipment, but also on tariffication principles. For example where local calls are free of charge, as has been the case historically in parts of the United States and Canada, the statistical importance of telecommunications income in GDP may be less. Similarly in many countries telecommunications charges have not kept pace with the consumer price index and in some cases have fallen.

It is important to note that growth of total telecommunications service income has for the majority of OECD countries been at a higher rate than growth of value-added in the service industry as a whole. The data for major OECD economies are shown as follows:

	Growth Rates $\frac{1984}{1974}$ in	
	Ratio of total telecommunications service income to GDP	Ratio of value-added in services to GDP
Canada	3.2	0.6
France	5.1	0.9
Germany	0.2	1.8
Italy	3.6	1.1
Japan	0.9	1.2
Sweden	1.2	1.3
United Kingdom	2.7	0.3
United States	1.2	0.6

Source: OECD.
Note: It is difficult to adjust telecommunications income to a value-added basis. Data are not therefore entirely comparable.

* Numbered tables in the text are prefixed by the roman numeral of their respective chapter. Tables in the statistical annex are numbered consecutively using only arabic numerals.

Real investment in telecommunications service infrastructure by common carriers in the OECD reached $54 billion in 1985, and has formed an important share of gross fixed capital formation in OECD countries (Table 2). Following the rapid build-up of the telecommunications system in the 1960s and 1970s the relative role of investment, which reached a peak in many countries at the end of the 1970s, diminished in the early 1980s. This can be illustrated by data from Japan:

	NTT investment GFCF
1963-67 3rd Plan	3.4 %
1968-72 4th Plan	3.1 %
1973-77 5th Plan	2.8 %
1978-82 6th Plan	2.3 %

However, given that many common carriers are in the process of digitalising and upgrading their networks investment is expected to show important improvements over the next few years (for example the Televerket in Sweden is planning to invest SKr 26.6 billion over 1988-90). Investment expenditure has also been boosted in the last several years in countries such as the United States, Japan and the United Kingdom, which have allowed competitive entry by new common carriers and which have begun to construct their own network facilities. Other countries, as well, where the telecommunications infrastructure is lagging – such as Portugal and Turkey – have recently planned extensive investment in building-up and replacing the existing infrastructure[6].

The investment role of private enterprises in telecommunications has been increasing significantly with the growth of data communications, and may be expected to continue to do so, as liberalisation in telecommunications progresses and as new services become available. However, in this case it is becoming increasingly difficult to classify the equipment as communications-related or computer-related.

Important differences exist among Member countries in terms of real per capita investment in telecommunications services by common carriers and regarding trends in this variable (Table 11). The lumpiness of investment makes it difficult to determine trends. Several countries stand out as showing, over the last few years, important increases in investment, in particular Austria, Germany, Sweden, Switzerland and Turkey. The relative distribution of investment between the United States, Japan and the EEC (10) has remained fairly constant over the period.

Investment by common carriers : 3-year moving average

(Million US$ constant 1980 price levels and exchange rates)

	1975-77	1977-79	1979-81	1981-83	1983-85
United States	15 557	17 927	18 683	16 523	15 984
Japan	6 529	6 822	6 637	6 646	6 753
EEC[10]	16 219	17 155	17 778	18 093	18 948
Germany	3 602	3 996	5 091	5 649	6 337
France	4 522	5 598	5 190	4 567	4 535
United Kingdom	2 968	2 494	2 746	2 837	2 792
Total OECD	46 593	50 121	52 824	52 544	49 866

OECD telecommunications equipment exports account for 1 per cent of total OECD manufacturing trade. In 1985 telecommunications equipment exports represented 1 per cent or more of manufacturing exports for only 7 OECD countries, and only represented a significant proportion of manufacturing trade for Sweden (4.1 per cent). Telecommunications equipment imports, as a percentage of total manufacturing imports, has averaged 1 per cent and over, in 1985 for Australia, Finland, Iceland, Ireland, New Zealand, Norway, Sweden, Turkey and the United States. Given data problems and the methodology used in bilateral valuation of international calls it is difficult to relate international telecommunications traffic revenue to trade in services, but some national data indicate a significant growing deficit in net payments, for example, by United States carriers for overseas (excluding Canada and Mexico) telephone traffic flows:

Net dollar flow in telephone traffic payments:

$ million

1975	1980	1983	1984
−83.7	−311.4	−799.9	−926.4

Source: Federal Communications Commission.

For certain countries, such as the United States, given the significant amount of multinational business activity and the relatively large number of immigrants in its population, one would expect the number of outgoing calls to continue to exceed incoming calls.

OECD production of telecommunications equipment is equivalent to about 0.5 to 0.7 per cent of total OECD GDP, varying slightly between producing countries but significantly higher in Sweden at around 1.2 per cent. In terms of employment, it is worth noting that U.S. Department of Commerce estimates, indicate that the communications industry widely defined (along with computing and office automation) has created 27 per cent of new jobs in high technology industries over 1979-83, and is expected to create the most jobs over the 1983-87 period.

Available data on consumer expenditure indicate that household spending on communications services forms only a small percentage of total consumption expenditure and that this ratio has grown but at different rates. Data (table I-1) for Japan, the United Kingdom, Germany and France, illustrate these trends. In the case of the United Kingdom the trend rate of real consumer expenditure on telecommunications services was at 7.2 per cent, over 1975-85 compared to 1.9 per cent for all household expenditure.

Microeconomic Role

Technological developments in computers, communications and microelectronics have led to significant declines in the cost of information processing[7], in network capability and communications costs. A range of new services has emerged and many traditional services have been transformed based on the merging of computer and communications technologies and their enhanced capabilities. For certain services, such as banking, financial services, tourism, airlines, etc., telecommunications have profoundly altered their production structures and now constitute the basic infrastructure for the provision of such services. It has been argued that an important determinant for the geographical location of the high value-added activities of the future will be the telecommunications structure given that these activities are communications-intensive[8].

Table I-1. Household spending for communications services as percentage of total consumption expenditure

(In percent)

Japan

	1974	1979	1984
Mail	0.1	0.1	0.2
Telegrammme and telephone calls	1.2	1.8	1.8
Broadcasting	0.2	0.2	0.3
Expenditure on total communications	1.5	2.2	2.2

United Kingdom

	1975	1980	1985
Telecommunications services	1.1	1.4	1.7

Germany

	1981	1982	1985
Post, Telegraph and Telephone			
Type 1 household*	2.6	2.5	2.5
Type 2 household*	1.7	1.7	1.7

France

	1970	1980	1984
Telecommunications and Post	0.6	1.1	1.2

Sources: *Japan*, Ministry of Posts and Telecommunications, Communications in Japan: *United Kingdom*, CSO, National Income and Expenditure 1985;
Germany, Statistisches Bundesamt, Statistisches Jahrbuch; *France*, INSEE, La Consommation des ménages en 1984.
* Type 1 household is a low income level household of 2 persons, and Type 2 a medium income level household with 4 persons.

Reliable data are not available to indicate the dependence of different industries on telecommunications. The annual survey of the International Communications Association of the United States attempts to estimate telecommunications expenditure as a percentage of industry operating expenses in some sectors of the United States:

	1985 in percent
Retailing (non-food)	3.02%
Banks	2.33
Office equipment/computers	1.55
Financial (non-banks)	1.38
Universities/Non-profit institutions	1.30
Service industries	1.05
Manufacturing	0.81

Source: International Communications Association, 1985 Telecommunications Expense Survey.

The data do not reflect the fact that without efficient communications many of the service sectors could not function properly and would be severely constrained in their service offerings. As OECD economies continue to shift towards service-based economic structures, the relative importance of communications services may be expected to grow. Indicative of this trend is, for example, growth in activity by intra-sectoral groupings such as the Society for World Wide Interbank Financial Telecommunications where the average daily traffic volume has increased from 121 000 messages in 1978 to approximately 650 000 messages by 1985. Projections of network terminating points, and for installed terminals, also tend to confirm the continued growth potential[9]. Expected growth in the number of installed computers, many of which are increasingly being interconnected in networks, is indicative of the growing role of information in the economy and the importance of communications networks:

Number of computer installations in the world

(Units)

1980	1982	1984	1986	1990
1 986 670	7 028 080	24 350 150	45 553 910	91 885 300

Source: IDC: All categories of computers included.

It should be stressed that there are already wide differences in the number and use of data terminals per number of employees in different countries. Estimates for the European Community have indicated that Luxembourg and the United Kingdom, for example, have nearly twice as many data terminals per employee as Germany[10].

The telecommunications industry is also important as a provider of infrastructure and services for manufacturing sectors and especially as a key factor in computer integrated manufacturing, in office automation and in linking stand-alone automation systems through local area networks. The trend in manufacturing production processes towards automation and the interlinkage of automation systems on the factory-floor and between plants, is playing a growing role in terms of future industrial competitiveness. Efficient and competitively-priced communications will have important implications for firm performance.

Widespread usage of communications networks by manufacturing and service industries may have important effects on the functioning of markets in OECD economies. For example, easier access to market information, lower costs and faster dissemination of such information may help reduce market imperfections attributable to incomplete or insufficient information processes. Also, more rapid adjustment of markets to changing supply/demand signals in terms of output and price can be expected. Inventory investment requirements have already been reduced in many sectors through use of communications networks in controlling raw material, intermediate input and final product inventories. Consideration needs to be given as to how such developments will impact on macroeconomic policy.

The telecommunications industry can also be considered as an important market in its own right for equipment, parts and software services. For example, the "semiconductor intensity" of the United States telecommunications equipment industry[11] is estimated to increase from 12.5 per cent in 1983 to 18.4 per cent by 1988[12]. In Japan, the communications equipment industry accounted for 8.1 per cent of the demand for integrated circuits in 1984 up from 6.9 per cent in 1980. The development of Integrated Services Digital Networks (ISDN) is expected to create significant growth for integrated circuits, specific to ISDN standards. In terms of innovation the telecommunications, industry is also recognised as a driving force for the development of information technology, electronic, microelectronic and communications technology. The impact of these technologies is widespread throughout all economic sectors.

In terms of employment, the shift in the occupational composition of employment in OECD countries towards an 'information' workforce has already been well documented[13]. Changes in the occupational structure, it has been argued, are based on the merging of computer and communications technology, which has facilitated changes in the manufacturing process away from material processing, has assisted in the shift in employment to the service sector away from manufacturing and agriculture and in structural changes in the service sector itself. Continued adjustment in occupational strutures may be expected on the basis of existing trends in information technology and its diffusion.

NOTES AND REFERENCES

1. Approximately 600 million sets in 1985.
2. The International Telecommunications Union defines a 'main line' as "a telephone line connecting the subscriber's terminal equipment to the public switched network and which has a dedicated part in the telephone exchange equipment".
3. The substantial disparities in world telecommunications development are reflected in the table below:

	Percentage of world main lines	Main Lines per 100 population
Europe	40.12	20.93
Africa	1.22	0.91
Asia	25.33	3.34
North and Central America	28.08	28.60
South America	3.33	5.02
Oceania	1.88	29.63
	100.00	

Source: STET.

4. Frost and Sullivan, "Advanced Business Communications in the US, 1986-1996", estimate that companies in the United States spent about $70 billion on communications services in 1986 and about $20 billion on customer premises equipment. Estimates for total expenditures in 1996 on telecommunications, computer and information services and equipment is put at $200 billion.
5. The International Telecommunications Union/OECD Development Centre joint project on Telecommunications and Development indicates, for example, that a 10 per cent rise in the number of telephones per 100 population over a 5-year period contributed in the 7 following years to a rise in average per capita income of 3 per cent.
6. Portugal, for example, plans to spend about Esc 170 billion over the next decade for digital switching.
7. The following changes in time and cost requirements for the treatment of 1 700 operations representing one million instructions have been estimated by IBM:

	1955	1965	1975	1984/85
Information processing	375 seconds	29 seconds	4 seconds	1 second
Cost	14.54	0.47	0.20	0.07

8. Commission for the European Communities, COM(86)547 Final, Proposal for a Council Regulation on a Community Action in the field of Telecommunications Technologies RACE, Brussels, 29th October 1986.

9. For example, the National Plan for Telecommunications in Italy, 1985-1994, projects the following growth in the number of terminals:

	1984	1994
Telex subscribers	64 000	120 000
Data transmission terminals	137 000	522 000
Facsimile terminals	8 000	40 000
Teletex terminals	700	140 000
Videotex terminals	2 000	250 000
Value-added services : terminals	–	250 000

10. Eurodata Foundation (1984)

11. Measured by the value of semiconductor purchases over total telecommunications equipment value.

12. Dataquest estimates.

13. See for example: Porat, M.U., The Information Economy, United States Department of Commerce, Office of Telecommunications, Washington, D.C., 1977; OECD, Information Activities, Electronics and Telecommunications Technologies, Paris, 1981.

Chapter II

STRUCTURAL CHARACTERISTICS AND CHANGE IN TELECOMMUNICATIONS SERVICES

Previous to 1984 the telecommunications service industry in most OECD countries had been structured on the basis of a monopoly: state-owned or privately-owned and state regulated. The basis for this, centred around the argument that cost advantages in production were such in telecommunications that it was more efficient for one firm to serve the market, that is, the industry was a natural monopoly. Secondly, public welfare considerations which have viewed telecommunications as a public service based on the principle of universal service provision required, it was argued, a monopoly rather than competitive structure.

Arguments regarding the extent to which telecommunications is, or is not, a natural monopoly and particularly whether universal service is possible in market structures other than on the basis of a monopoly, remain key in ongoing debates in the OECD area. However, sweeping changes in technology, the availability for potential new services and new service concepts and customer requirements have placed different perspectives on these arguments. Differences in regulatory approaches to deal with the potential services, which have become available as a result of the merging in computer and communications technologies, have led to differences in the degree of market access between countries leading increasingly to international friction in this area. Digitalisation, which is providing a single language to handle all information (voice, data, graphics, imagery) and is enhancing transmission capacity and speed, has led to increased blurring of boundaries in communications and information processing. The deregulation of market structures which has occurred in some countries is still too recent to effectively judge its effects. Before entering into some of the issues it is first necessary to review network size and growth and the performance of service providers.

1. Network Size and Growth

The number of subscriber main lines in the OECD area increased from 184.5 million in 1974 to about 318 million by 1985 – a growth rate of 5.1 per cent per annum. There exist, however, important differences in network development among Member countries as measured by main lines per capita (Table 3) or in terms of telephone sets per capita (Table 4). Sweden is significantly in advance of other OECD countries in terms of main lines and telephone sets per capita. Countries such as Germany, France, Japan and the United

Kingdom despite their relatively advanced industrial structures and economic weight, are considerably behind Sweden in network development when measured either in terms of main lines per capita or telephone sets per capita. Sustained high levels of investment over the rest of this decade would be required for these countries to attain penetration rates equivalent to those of Sweden, or even those of the United States – growth rates which for some of these countries would exceed historical growth experienced during the 1970s when infrastructure investment was at its peak. There are also important variations in country distribution of main lines between residential and business subscribers. In countries with a weak, but developing, service infrastructure, the percentage of residential main lines is increasinig in relative importance, while the role of residential main lines is declining relatively in countries with a well developed infrastructure.

Important differences also exist in the size of networks as shown below in comparing data for major countries. The dominant size of the United States network – linked with the openness of its telecommunications market – explains the attractiveness of this market for foreign equipment and service providers. In contrast, although as a whole the European Community network is nearly equivalent in size to the United States, the individual size of the major European country networks are only one-fifth that of the United States and half that of Japan. The United States, Japan and the EEC[10] account for 83 per cent of OECD telecommunications main lines.

Millions of main lines

	1983	1984	1985	% of total OECD in 1985
United States	111.0	114.0	117.0	36.8
Japan	42.4	43.8	45.4	14.3
EEC (10)	92.2	98.2	102.2	32.1
Germany	23.5	24.6	25.6	8.0
France	19.3	22.1	23.0	7.2
United Kingdom	19.5	20.2	20.9	6.6
Italy	15.6	16.5	17.4	5.5
Canada	10.5	11.8	12.5	3.9
Spain	8.4	8.9	9.3	2.9
OECD Total	290.3	302.0	318.3	

Each of the individual regional holding companies in the United States has a larger network, as measured by main lines, than most OECD countries (with the exception of Japan, United Kingdom, Germany, France and Italy)[1].

Universal Service

In view of the mandate of telecommunications administrations the first question which needs to be raised is to what extent have telecommunications administrations been successful in providing a universal telecommunications service in terms of making the telephone accessible to all households. The wide variation which exists in the number of telephone sets per capita in the OECD and the wide variation which exists *within* countries in telephone penetration in major cities and smaller towns (Table 5) indicate that important differences still exist in telephone penetration rates[2]. The uneven rate of development in telecommunications infrastructure, regionally within countries and nationally across the OECD, is apparent not only in basic services but in the availability of new business services and also in modern facilities such as digital switching and transmission.

Perhaps the most interesting revelation of penetration rate data is that telephone administrations in many Member countries have, since the postwar era, been incredibly slow in implementing a concept which has now become their raison d'être – it is sufficient to note that the telephone line density of Sweden and the United States in *1974* had not been reached by any other OECD country ten years later[3]. Many OECD countries have in fact only in the last decade taken significant steps to build up their networks – resulting in part from a neglect of their responsibilities prior to the early 1970s. For many of these countries, data on waiting lists for telephones, and active private markets selling connections in urban areas, indicate significant pent-up demand during this period. To what extent private network providers in a competitive environment would have been more efficient is a hypothetical question. It needs to be recognized that often governments themselves, by depriving PTTs of funding (either by not allowing external borrowing, through tariff policies, or requiring cross-subsidisation of postal services), prevented telephone administrations from meeting their responsibilities.

Investments since the 1970s by PTTs have, in many cases, brought telephone penetration closer to notional saturation levels. Data on waiting lists for main lines (see Table 6) show for many countries an important improvement in response time to meet unfulfilled demand. Nevertheless important differences still exist in average waiting time both among countries and within countries. For example estimates by the Bureau Européen des Unions de Consommateurs indicate an average waiting time for a new connection within the European Community ranging from 4.5 years in Greece, 6 months in Spain, 1 to 2 months in Germany and 2 to 3 weeks in Denmark. Within individual countries there is also a marked contrast; for example, 2 days in Paris compared to an average of 3 weeks for the rest of France, or 1 to 4 months in urban Italy compared to 6 to 8 months in rural Italy. The considerable improvement which has occurred (since the early 1970s) in telephone penetration rates is reflected in the data for France (below) which had during the period an exceptionally high investment rate:

**Penetration of telephones by households
according to socio-professional category in France**
(Percentages)

	1979	1981	1984	1985
Farmers	54.1	72.0	90.5	94.1
Company owners/Managers	82.9	93.6	105.6	107.4
Liberal professions/senior executives	86.5	94.2	100.6	101.1
Middle Executive	76.2	87.4	94.7	98.9
Employees and other categories	48.9	69.6	86.2	90.1
Workers	35.9	57.1	80.7	82.3
Unemployed	43.4	60.3	78.7	83.5

Source: Direction Générale des Télécommunications, Statistiques 1985.

The second aspect regarding network growth is that differences in relative degrees of liberalisation have not been important, at least as regards the development of the telephone service[4]. There is insufficient evidence to indicate whether private regulated monopolies were more effective than public monopolies in all cases in providing basic telecommunications services – on the contrary the data for Sweden, Switzerland and some Nordic countries indicate a higher penetration of basic services than the United States. Thirdly, in comparing, at the international level, the cost to the consumer of telephone services it is difficult to draw any general conclusions except that national network sizes and the *relative* charges paid by consumers in different countries are not highly related. The notion of the existence of economies of scale in the supply of telecommunications services, in network growth, development and network control, could be interpreted to imply that there should be a closer correlation between relative network size and relative customer charges in that differences in performance should be reflected in costs and therefore prices.

Recognising that there are methodological difficulties in undertaking international comparisons of relative service costs, the data in Tables II-1*(a)* and *(b)* are consistent nevertheless, showing the lowest average monthly charges for Sweden, Spain and the

Table II-1. Comparative telecommunications service charges

(a)   Index of average monthly telephone bill per:

	Household	Company
Sweden	100	100
Netherlands	113	100
Spain	143	181
France	165	215
Germany	183	210
Canada	194	200
United States	198	268
Switzerland	204	262
United Kingdom	210	283
Italy	236	343
Japan	279	352

Source: Logica (1985).

(b)   International Comparison of Telephone Bills

	Residential	Business
Sweden	61	45
Spain	74	56
Netherlands	88	66
Australia	107	97
Canada (Bell)	60	99
United Kingdom	100	100
West Germany	132	102
Japan	140	108
United States (New York and AT&T)	106	116
Italy	129	119
France	174	123

Source: BT Supplementary Report 1986 (cited in Oftel, Review of British Telecom's Tariff Charges, November 1986).

Netherlands. Such data must, however, be interpreted with care given that prices may or may not be cost-based, and therefore relative differences in charges may in such cases reflect different pricing policies, network costs or policies regarding cross-subsidisation.

Operational Performance

It is useful as a broad indicator to examine relative performance by telecommunications service providers. Such international comparisons, though useful in indicating broad differences in performance and relative shifts in such performance over time, need to be undertaken with caution in that differences in market structures, pricing and accounting procedures, employment policies[5], as well as relative degrees of use of new switching and transmission technologies, can bias comparisons. Data on operational performance in telecommunications services (Table II-2) do not allow for specific conclusions to be made as to the importance or lack of importance of overall network size. Switzerland's operational expenditure per main line and per unit traffic is comparable to these ratios for the United States, despite significant network size differences. The data rather reflect the diversity of results of common carriers of different sizes and servicing markets with different character-istics. Similarly, revenue data provide a mixed picture which may reflect pricing and accounting policies rather than operational performance per se (Table II-3). The data also indicate that it is possible to provide basic telecommunications services efficiently and profitably at a very small scale – witness Hull City or the relative performance of Telecom Canada (a co-operative of ten separate regional carriers which are financially autonomous and serve a range of market sizes) at half the size of British Telecom or one-quarter the size of NTT in Japan. Significant improvements have occurred in most OECD countries in network capital-labour ratios, as measured by number of main lines per staff. As well, operational expenditure per unit traffic have tended to decline. The data cast doubts on PTT assertions that a single carrier can lead to substantial cost saving by integrating responsibility of network and service planning and control. Some relationships may change if other measurement criteria are used, but it is doubtful if the main thrust of the above conclusions would be altered. It is worth noting that revenue per employee and per access line by the North American carriers tends to be higher than for other OECD countries[6].

Revenue

Total revenue from telecommunications services which in current dollars totalled $199 billion in 1985 has grown in real terms at an annual average rate of 5.1 per cent during the period 1974-85 (Table 7). The United States accounts for about 45 per cent of this income, and the EEC (10) 30 per cent. Significant differences exist among OECD countries in terms of per capita telecommunications service income and growth in this variable (Table 7). Claims that economies of scale, reduce costs, which in turn may lead to increased demand, would tend to imply that network size should be reflected in per capita service income and its growth. In general, however, the level in per capita telecommunications service income reflects the level of development in the network as measured in per capita main line or telephone sets per capita.

Growth in telephone traffic (Table 8) has been particularly high in countries which have recently developed their networks from a relatively low level (e.g. Ireland, Greece, New Zealand), but has also remained high in countries with a well developed network – 4.7 per cent annual average over 1974-84 in the United States, 4.6 per cent in Sweden, 4 per cent in Canada. Per capita traffic has also shown important increases in countries with developed

Table II-2. Comparative data on common carriers
(Expressed in constant US$ at 1980 prices and exchange rates)

	Revenue per main line		Operational expenditure per main line		Operational expenditure per unit traffic[1]		Main lines per employee		Index of network sizes* for 1985 (US = 100)
	1974	1985	1974	1985	1974	1985	1974	1985	
Australia	$544	$568	$236	$264	0.22	0.28	38	69	5.4
Belgium	487	530	316	234	0.40	–	60	111	2.6
Canada	473	561	231	336	0.09	–	89	125	10.7
France	1 018	633	559	273	0.13	0.08	52	138	19.7
Germany	1 028	620	475	158	0.42	0.01	64	120	21.9
Italy	441	420	392	225	0.36	0.21	93	158	14.9
Japan	370+	443	98	93	–	–	93+	141	38.8
Netherlands	621	462	319	238	0.30	0.23	123	202	5.0
Spain	409	370	104	88	–	–	67	130	8.0
Sweden	425	477	274	323	0.07	0.06	107	125	4.5
Switzerland	706	741	406	337	0.12	0.09	147	179	2.8
United Kingdom	505+	612	–	427	–	0.36	52+	89	17.9
United States	587	736	281	435	0.10	–	89	169	100.0

Source: ITU/OECD.
* Based on main lines
+ 1975 data used for 1974
1. Traffic measured in charged calls except France and Sweden measured in pulses, and United Kingdom measure in number of calls.

Table II-3. **Comparative network revenue data for 1984**

(U.S.$ at current exchange rates)

	Revenue per employee	Revenue per access line	Operating income per Employee	Main line	Exchange access lines ('000)
Telecom Australia	41 818	–	3 059	–	–
British Columbia Tel.Co.	66 799	601	17 244	155	1 475
GTE (telephone operations)	88 009	755	25 281	217	12 000
Germany (Bundespost)	52 654	439	–	–	24 900
France (DGT)	50 329	378	4 475	34	22 100
Italy (SIP)	58 335	272	29 649	138	16 521
Japan (NTT)	59 562	441	5 083	38	42 879
Sweden (Televerket)	42 232	365	6 688	58	5 128
British Telecom	43 299	507	10 609	124	20 065
Hull City (U.K.)	34 114	187	11 012	60	131
Telecom Canada*	72 657	615	21 213	180	11 156
(Bell)	79 688	581	27 507	201	6 823

Source: Annual Reports.
* A co-operative of ten major carriers in Canada.

communications systems with some important exceptions, namely the United Kingdom and Germany, where per capita traffic is extremely low. In several countries calling rates have declined, or remained flat, so that growth in traffic resulted from increasing expansion of the network:

Calls per main line

	1974	1983	1984	1985
Canada	2 627	2 823	2 882	2 781
France (pulses)	4 172	3 759	3 573	3 599
Germany	1 142	1 079	1 074	1 079
Italy	1 092	993	1 053	1 072
Sweden (pulses)	4 192	5 134	5 262	5 509
United Kingdom	1 122	1 138	1 138	1 187
United States	2 864	3 522	3 144	–

Source: Derived from ITU data. As noted in Table 8 differences exist among countries in measurement of traffic.

High calls per main line in Canada and the United States may reflect the use of flat rate charges instead of measured service charges[7].

For nearly all telecommunications administrations, income from telephone calls accounts for 50 per cent or more of total telecommunications income (Table 9). Other income sources include connection charges, income from annual rentals, public telegramme service income, telex income and from services such as data and facsimile transmission services. It is interesting to examine the distribution of income by type of service for some major OECD economies (Table II-4). Annual rental of equipment is a particularly important income source explaining why many telecommunications administrations are reluctant to reduce their monopoly equipment supply positions. The proportion of rental income in total income in the United States is high relative to other countries reflecting pricing decisions favouring the use

Table II-4. **Percentage distribution of income by source from telecommunications**

	Connection charges			Annual rentals			Public telegramme service			Telex service			Other income (data/facsimile)		
	1974	1984	1985	1974	1984	1985	1974	1984	1985	1974	1984	1985	1974	1984	1985
Germany	1.4	0.7	0.7	25.8	25.4	25.2	1.2	0.4	0.4	3.9	3.2	3.1	5.5	6.8	7.3
United States	–	–	–	47.5	32.4	–	0.5	0.2	0.1	1.2	0.8	0.6	1.0	7.8	12.0
France	2.6	1.1	–	15.4	14.3	13.2*	2.2	0.01	–	3.8	2.4	2.3	16.4	19.8	19.6
Italy	3.7	3.5	3.3	18.0	21.1	21.3	4.0	1.4	1.5	2.4	4.5	5.7	0.8	5.4	4.1
Japan	8.6	2.7[1]	2.7	18.7	24.2[1]	24.0	1.1	0.9	0.8	2.3	1.5	1.4	9.4	11.2	12.3
United Kingdom	3.3	2.7[2]	–	28.5	33.9	33.2	5.0	1.2	–	5.4	4.2	4.2	3.1	8.1	8.7
Sweden	4.8	6.9	7.4	19.3	21.7	20.7	1.5	0.3	0.3	2.2	3.9	4.1	6.1	10.7	11.8
Switzerland	–	–	–	23.9	24.6	23.8	2.5	0.8	0.1	6.7	6.8	6.5	16.1	6.9	6.7

1. 1983.
2. 1982.
* Includes connection charge and maintenance.

27

of subscriber charges with unlimited local calls in most areas. Rental income (excluding subscriber charges) should be considerably reduced from 1984 onwards, in view of the significant number of consumers who purchased their telephone sets from AT&T. Connection charge income has shown a relative decline with the exception of Sweden as has telegramme income. An important income growth area for most countries is in data, facsimile and other services. However, if the growth in these services occurs in private networks, as in the United States, a good comparison between countries cannot be made.

A key factor in network development and revenue growth has been the fact that only a small percentage of customers are responsible for an important percentage of revenue and revenue growth and network usage[8]. For example, in *France* main lines to business, accounting for 20 per cent of total main lines, are responsible for 52 per cent of total telephone traffic; 2 per cent of main lines are responsible for 20 per cent of total traffic. In the *United States* 4 per cent of users account for 50-60 per cent of common carrier revenues, while the remainder of demand is very diffuse (households, small business users). For long-distance alone this concentration is much more marked – it is estimated that 10 per cent of residence customers account for about one-half of all residence interstate messages, while 10 per cent of businesses account for about three-quarters of business interstate messages and 1 per cent of business locations account for 40 per cent of all business interstate message toll service revenues[9]. It is these major users who are the main customers for new services. But it is also these users who are demanding greater freedom of choice, flexibility in service supply and price competition, which is not usually provided in a monopoly service structure.

The high debt ratios of many telecommunications administrations, linked with the need to undertake investment in digital equipment and transmission, (see section below) and coupled with slow growth in the main revenue source of PTTs (basic voice communications), is expected to have important consequences. Local telephone tariffs which have been adjusted significantly in several countries over the last few years are unlikely for economic (and political) reasons, to be able to sustain continuous increases[10]. Increased operating efficiency is unlikely on its own to be sufficient to overcome this slower revenue growth. The reaction by telephone administrations has been to try, in some cases, to maintain and/or extend control over telecommunications service areas which are experiencing rapid growth (data transmission, facsimile, mobile cellular telephony, value-added services, etc.) Mobile cellular telephony is thus considered as a common carrier service in many countries provided by government-sanctioned monopolies. Such control has in some cases been exercised through control over equipment supply and/or installation (e.g. modems, facsimile machines).

Constraints on the development of these new markets by monopoly telecommunications service providers – in particular by limiting user choice – may dampen revenue growth prospects in the very areas that service providers are counting on to overcome their revenue constraints. The economic rationale to solve this dilemma of telecommunications administrations would suggest opening the telecommunications market to increased competition and allowing a range of new services to emerge driven by the market. Market dynamics, in such an event, could be expected to rapidly stimulate demand and provide beneficial spillover effects to national networks in terms of increased usage and revenues. The rapid development and growth of telecommunications based information service markets in the United Kingdom and Japan, for example, following liberalisation in those markets, attests to the ability of the market to stimulate growth for all participants in the market, including the common carrier. However, the reaction of many European monopoly telephone administrations reflects a deeply embedded scepticism as to the dynamics of the market and its ability to meet user requirements efficiently. Rather, there is a preference for a planned phase-in of new services.

It is important to note the regional concentration in telecommunications traffic, and revenue, in most countries. For example, in France the Paris basin region (Ile-de-France) accounts for close to one-third of telephony traffic. Such concentration is often reinforced by investment decisions of telecommunications administrations through geographical concentration of investment in new services and technologically advanced facilities. There is also a considerable geographical concentration of traffic at the international level[11].

Any analysis of the service sector is incomplete if it is not stressed that telephone services will continue to provide the bulk of revenue and to play the main role in the telecommunications service industry despite high growth in data communications and in new services. The structure of networks will continue to be based around telephony at least until the end of the century.

Investment

Telecommunications investment by common carriers in the OECD increased in real terms at a rate of 2 percent over 1975 to 1985. The pattern of investment (Table 10) reflects the network expansion of the 1970s with most countries reaching an investment peak in the 1979-81 or 1981-83 periods. A subsequent slow-down in network expansion is now being followed by increased investment particular as countries are moving to modernise their networks. Significant differences also exist in per capita investment in telecommunications services by common carriers (Table 11). In particular, Switzerland and Norway have had a high level of per capita investment, and in recent years Sweden, Germany, Austria and France.

The rapid investment in networks in the 1970s changed considerably the telephone administrations' financial structure, particularly as regards debt:

- In France the DGT (Direction Générale des Télécommunications) had at the end of 1985 a high debt ratio: approximately FF 125 billion, costing FF 16.4 billion to service and equivalent to 19 per cent of annual turnover;
- The Australian Telecom Commission has a long-term debt equivalent to 39 per cent of revenue in 1984 and 42 per cent in 1983;
- In Sweden, the Televerket's ratio of long-term debt to total income has risen from 1 per cent in 1979/80 to 13.5 per cent by 1983/84.

In view of the expected high investment requirements for integrated service digital networks, it is important that telecommunications administrations should not be constrained financially. Adequate access to financial instruments and autonomy in financial administration may therefore be an important requirement.

There has been a trend towards investment shifting away from network expansion to network modernisation that is replacement investment. Much of this investment for digital transmission and switching systems is in effect capacity-augmenting given the ability of digital systems to handle more information. For certain types of facility investment it may be expected that per unit capacity investment will decline, e.g. fibre-optic cables can use existing ducts to a large extent reducing cable-laying costs.

Telecommunications investment, at different times and in different countries, has also been severely constrained directly by the governments themselves. These arose from policies which prohibited telecommunications administrations from borrowing on capital markets, from requiring surplus telecommunications revenues to be used to subsidise postal losses, or to be transferred to central government funds and through constraints on charges. For example, in Italy SIP had for many years been allowed only limited increases in charges and for some years no increases. This policy undertaken for macroeconomic stabilization purposes had obvious and severe impacts on the development of the Italian telecommunications system. Similarly, in Germany, telecommunications revenue of the Deutsche Bundespost, has been diverted over a long period to cover losses on the postal side and in banking services (GIRO). The transfers by the French PTT to the central government Treasury and to finance industrial policy initiatives of the government with regard to the filière électronique have been substantial[12] – equivalent to about 923 French francs per main line. A 25 per cent tariff increase by the French PTT in 1984 was imposed in effect as a fiscal measure allowing the government to reduce (or prevent the need to increase) taxes in other areas. Such measures may prevent the efficient allocation of funds as well as constrain telecommunications administrations from reducing debt ratios and adjusting tariffs.

France : PTT transfers to central government
(Billions of French Francs)

	1982	1983	1984	1985	1986 (estimate)
Total	2.8	2.4	8.4	18.0	20.3
of which: for filière électronique	–	0.4	3.4	6.5	5.0

It must be recognised that OECD Member governments have different social goals. However, a choice needs to be made as to whether it is more efficient to support other economic or social goals directly, or to allow telecommunications administrations to implement social cross-subsidies within their rate structures, or require administrations to directly subsidise other related industrial goals through operating revenues. Governments should not use as an argument for maintaining telecommunications monopolies, the requirement to provide and protect universal service, when they themselves have, at times and to an important extent, retarded the ability of telecommunications administrations to provide such a service by imposing goals which are not service-related.

Service Employment

Total employment in telecommunications services, that is, by common carriers, increased at an annual average rate of 0.8 per cent over 1974 to 1985 for the OECD as a whole. Relative changes in telecommunications employment for major countries and the relative importance of such employment is shown in the table below[13]:

Telecommunications service employment : 1984

	Growth 1984/1974	As percentage of	
		Total employment	Total service employment
United States*	1.20	0.96	1.40
Japan	0.25	0.56	1.00
Germany	0.89	0.82	1.58
France	3.30	0.78	1.35
United Kingdom*	–0.02	1.01	1.59
Italy	1.00	0.52	1.02
Canada*	2.80	1.06	1.53
EEC (10)	1.10	0.79	1.38
OECD	1.20	0.79	1.33

* 1974-1983.

Employment growth, despite being positive (with the exception of the United Kingdom) does not compare favourably with growth in employment in service industries as a whole. The increase in labour productivity, occurred through factors such as automated dialing (both local and long-distance) and less maintenance as a result of the increase in electronic systems. It is fairly evident that increasing service efficiency and facility modernisation will have negative employment effects[14]. On the other hand there is an important growth potential in high skill areas in the new service areas.

An important stumbling block in the adjustment of telecommunications service structures in certain countries is based on the reticence of employees in state-owned telecommunications administrations to alter their employment status from civil servants to that of private employees. Such a change wouldtend to occur if the organisational structure of telecommunications administrations altered from a government agency to a public corporation. The relevant telecommunications labour unions are in particular concerned that a change in employment status would allow for, and lead to, an important reduction in employment. In France and Germany, for example, the telecommunications unions have clearly stated their opposition to organisational changes which would alter their present status.

2. The Restructuring of the Telecommunications Service Industry

The last five years can be viewed as the era of adjustment in the telecommunications service industry in the OECD. The next five years will reflect the imperative of many industrialised OECD countries to catch up in the telecommunications service offerings of their major trading partners, as a result of delayed adjustment in the telecommunications service industry.

The adjustment process in the telecommunications service industry toward greater liberalisation has been most profound in recent years in the United States, Japan and the United Kingdom. Changes have occurred in other OECD countries – in some cases of a marginal nature, in others of longer-term significance – but not to the extent of the former three countries. The changes which have occurred in the United States, Japan and the United Kingdom were of different degrees and reflect differences in national structures. Liberalisation of the telecommunications service framework was also undertaken by these countries for different reasons.

The adjustment process has also differed in terms of rapidity of introduction. Whereas in the United States liberalisation began in 1956 with the Hush-A-Phone decision (see Annex II), in Japan changes undertaken were rapid. In the United States changes in the industry often appeared not to reflect well thought-out strategies often because of conflicts in policy priorities among the different participating institutions. The Modification of Final Judgement (MFJ) court decision of 1982, based on antitrust proceedings aimed at constraining AT&T's dominant position, led to the divestiture of AT&T and as a result provided a new set of ground rules for the industry's adjustment.

It is difficult to isolate any root cause which has led to changes in telecommunications services. Undoubtedly, however, technological changes played the major role in facilitating such changes. Various aspects in technological change can be highlighted:

- The development of alternative transmission facilities (microwave, satellite) which made it possible at a reasonable cost to by-pass common carrier networks;
- The merging of computer and communications technologies and the emergence of computer networking which opened up a wide range of business opportunities;

31

- The emergence of intelligent terminals and the ability of terminals to exchange information on-line;
- The basis of all these developments were developments in microelectronics which as a result of lower costs, miniaturisation, the ability to develop intelligence in a range of equipment and increased speed, created the information technology revolution, of which structural change in telecommunications is just one part.

Although the legal and economic structures of telecommunications have been brought into question by technology, it is in fact the business communities in all countries, and in particular large users of telecommunications services, which have been at the forefront in creating pressures for change. The attempt to grasp the opportunities provided by developments in information technology often clashed with static monopoly structures of telecommunications administrations.

This section will not review service policy changes in all OECD countries but highlight some of the most significant changes in recent years[15]. Further sections will review new service trends and their implications and the impact of service adjustment described in the paragraphs below.

It needs to be recalled that liberalisation in telecommunications regulations[16] can be viewed in terms of changes governing attachment of terminal equipment, changes governing network usage (leasing lines, resale of telephone line capacity, freedom in offering non-basic services) and facilities competition.

United States

The United States telecommunications service industry has a long history of structural change which has gradually liberalised the service framework by allowing increased competition (Annex II). Decisions such as Above 890 (1959) opened the door to competitive transmission facilities leading in 1969 to authorisation for MCI to set up a competing public facility. This policy became more generalised in 1971 when new entry by Specialized Common Carriers was allowed. In 1972 an 'open skies' policy allowed satellite facilities to be set up which would be competitive with wire facilities. The 1968 Carterfone decision began the process of liberalising terminal attachment which was not fully completed until 1977 (Second Order Registration) and 1980 (Second Computer Inquiry).

A major decision with regard to liberalisation in terms of services also derived from the Second Computer Inquiry of the Federal Communications Commission. The attempt to define what should be considered as a network service or as an enhanced or value-added service in terms of legal definitions, has not been successful, nor does it appear feasible. The effect however of allowing widespread service offerings by companies other than the common carrier provided a significant impetus to the growth of the service industry.

Changes started in 1980 accelerated in 1982 with the Modification of Final Judgement (MFJ) which divested AT&T of 22 local operating companies which were organised in 7 regional holding companies. Effective 1st January 1984, the United States service structure was characterised by:

- A competitive long-distance market serviced by the dominant carrier, AT&T, other common carriers, and specialised common carriers;
- Local exchange carriers which provide basic services and access by long-distance carriers to residential and business customers. These LATAs (Local Access and Transport Areas), of which some 1 400 exist, are subject to regulation by state Public Utilities Commissions and still maintain a monopoly;
- A differentiation between basic and enhanced service companies.

This change in structure has thus led to a differentiation between operating telephone companies and inter-exchange carriers which are concerned with routing traffic between LATAs.

The MFJ also applied the concept which had emerged from Computer Inquiry II of fully separate, that is arms-length, subsidiaries in other service areas for the divested AT&T and the Regional Holding Companies. This notion aimed at eliminating cross-subsidisation between basic and enhanced services, and therefore predatory practices by firms in a dominant position, has since been eliminated as an outcome of the Third Computer Inquiry. Restrictions still remain on Bell Operating Companies which prevent them offering certain services. During the course of the following year the issue of whether the regional Bell operating companies should be freed from such business restrictions will be under consideration. The BOCs are required to provide "equal access" (technically equivalent interconnections) to local telephone facilities at "cost-based rates".

The process of structural change in telecommunications services in the United States was unique in the OECD area given that the industry structure was based on a franchised private monopoly with an independent regulatory agency and a legal structure with a very strong anti-trust tradition. In several instances structural changes which increased telecommunications service competition resulted from judicial action and overturned regulatory (FCC) decisions which were not always responsive to change. Shifts in policy in the early 1980s by all branches of government has, however, been aimed at maximising competitive entry in the industry and emphasizing market forces.

United States policy has been characterised by the evolutionary process of change as the FCC attempted to define its regulatory role in a changing technological situation. At the same time it is apparent that there has been no co-ordinated or comprehensive attempt to enact a telecommunications policy at the level of Congress or by the Administration.

Japan

Prior to restructuring, the telecommunications service industry in Japan was divided between Nippon Telegraph and Telephone (NTT), providing local and domestic long-distance services, and KDD (Kokusai Denshi Denna) providing international services on its own facilities. This service structure was supervised by the Ministry of Posts and Telecommunications (MPT).

In Japan, growing business pressure for reform and more flexibility in telecommunications policy resulted at the political level in a recommendation by the Ad hoc Committee on Administrative Reform in 1982 for full scale divestiture and privatisation of NTT. Less drastic calls for reorganisation were supported by NTT itself in 1983 and by the Japan Federation of Economic Organizations. Conflict between the Ministry of Posts (MPT) and the Ministry of International Trade and Industry (MITI) given the latter's traditional responsibility for the computer industry also served as an impetus for reform in view of MITI's desire to foster value-added network services in the framework of market competition. United States pressure was also particularly strong in trying to open the VAN market to United States service providers[17].

It has been argued that MITI's intervention in telecommunications policy debate was premised on the fact that:

"In any new national economic system which will rely heavily on the use of sophisticated telecommunications systems integrated with computers, the agency which has the most influence on the computer/telecommunications industrial sector will be able to take the initiative in economic policy making"[18].

The MPT also recognised that Japan's telecommunications infrastructure, having attained a level of maturity, would need to respond to new demands for diversified and sophisticated telecommunications services which could be provided more effectively through competition.

Undoubtedly, in visions of an economy based on an information age, the wider economic benefit which could arise from a market-oriented telecommunications system, played an importance role in the adjustment of Japan's telecommunications service structure. This strong intervention by MITI was also unique relative to other OECD countries, where Economics and Industry ministries have been less active in attempting to change telecommunications structures, in order to allow their economies to take advantage of the potential offered by information-based systems and services in future years.

The Telecommunications Business Law which was enacted on 1st April 1985 had two aims:

- It introduced competition in domestic (local and toll) telecommunications by eliminating NTT's monopoly;
- A distinction was created between carriers that provide services using their own telecommunications facilities (Type I carriers) and those that lease such facilities (Type II carriers).

Carriers, unlike in the United States, are not classified by type of service provided. This effectively avoided entering into the debate on what constitutes a basic or an enhanced service. Type I carriers need MPT permission to provide services, and foreign-ownership is limited to one-third of shares, whereas for Type II services there are no restrictions on foreign ownership, and depending on whether Type II services are special or general, only registration or notification is required[19]. Liberalisation of value-added services had in fact begun in 1982 with the VAN for Small- and Medium-sized Business Act which allowed sharing of leased line capacity related to data processing, and allowed message-switching services (but not for third-party communications). Six Type I licences have been issued as of April 1987, four of which have begun operation. Consideration is also being given for a licence to operate international telecommunications services in competition with KDD.

In conjunction with the Business Law the Nippon Telegraph and Telephone Corporation Law reorganized NTT into a private company[20]. The right to authorise telecommunications terminals for connection with NTTs (or other) public communications network was transferred from the NTT to the Electrical Communication Terminal Equipment Examination Association and customers have been given the right to attach any equipment conforming to certain standards[21]. Rate regulation has remained with the Ministry of Posts and Telecommunications. NTT still has retained responsibility to provide universal service, but it is not clear to what extent this responsibility interacts with other structural changes and whether this responsibility can be used to maintain a dominant service position. In this regard Type I carriers may be required to pay access charges to NTT which help defray costs of local service. The Telecommunications Business Law will be reviewed by Parliament in 1988 and the NTT Corporation Law by 1990.

An important article in the Telecommunications Business Law concerns capacity. Thus (Article 10, paragraph 2):

"The introduction of the telecommunications business shall not result in a significant excess of telecommunications circuit facilities to be used for such business in all or in any part of the territory or route to be covered (serviced) by the telecommunications carrier"[22].

In an industry where capacity is normally provided to meet forecasted peak traffic needs and

OECD PUBLICATIONS, 2, rue André-Pascal, 75775 PARIS CEDEX 16 - No. 44325 1988
PRINTED IN FRANCE
(93 88 01 1) ISBN 92-64-13092-6

WHERE TO OBTAIN OECD PUBLICATIONS
OÙ OBTENIR LES PUBLICATIONS DE L'OCDE

ARGENTINA - ARGENTINE
Carlos Hirsch S.R.L.,
Florida 165, 4º Piso,
(Galeria Guemes) 1333 Buenos Aires
Tel. 33.1787.2391 y 30.7122

AUSTRALIA - AUSTRALIE
D.A. Book (Aust.) Pty. Ltd.
11-13 Station Street (P.O. Box 163)
Mitcham, Vic. 3132   Tel. (03) 873 4411

AUSTRIA - AUTRICHE
OECD Publications and Information Centre,
4 Simrockstrasse,
5300 Bonn (Germany)   Tel. (0228) 21.60.45
Gerold & Co., Graben 31, Wien 1   Tel. 52.22.35

BELGIUM - BELGIQUE
Jean de Lannoy,
avenue du Roi 202
B-1060 Bruxelles   Tel. (02) 538.51.69

CANADA
Renouf Publishing Company Ltd/
Éditions Renouf Ltée,
1294 Algoma Road, Ottawa, Ont. K1B 3W8
Tel: (613) 741-4333
Toll Free/Sans Frais:
Ontario, Quebec, Maritimes:
1-800-267-1805
Western Canada, Newfoundland:
1-800-267-1826
Stores/Magasins:
61 rue Sparks St., Ottawa, Ont. K1P 5A6
Tel: (613) 238-8985
211 rue Yonge St., Toronto, Ont. M5B 1M4
Tel: (416) 363-3171
Federal Publications Inc.,
301-303 King St. W.,
Toronto, Ontario M5V 1J5
Tel. (416)581-1552

DENMARK - DANEMARK
Munksgaard Export and Subscription Service
35, Nørre Søgade, DK-1370 København K
Tel. +45.1.12.85.70

FINLAND - FINLANDE
Akateeminen Kirjakauppa,
Keskuskatu 1, 00100 Helsinki 10   Tel. 0.12141

FRANCE
OCDE/OECD
Mail Orders/Commandes par correspondance :
2, rue André-Pascal,
75775 Paris Cedex 16
Tel. (1) 45.24.82.00
Bookshop/Librairie : 33, rue Octave-Feuillet
75016 Paris
Tel. (1) 45.24.81.67 or/ou (1) 45.24.81.81
Librairie de l'Université,
12a, rue Nazareth,
13602 Aix-en-Provence   Tel. 42.26.18.08

GERMANY - ALLEMAGNE
OECD Publications and Information Centre,
4 Simrockstrasse,
5300 Bonn   Tel. (0228) 21.60.45

GREECE - GRÈCE
Librairie Kauffmann,
28, rue du Stade, 105 64 Athens   Tel. 322.21.60

HONG KONG
Government Information Services,
Publications (Sales) Office,
Information Services Department
No. 1, Battery Path, Central

ICELAND - ISLANDE
Snæbjörn Jónsson & Co., h.f.,
Hafnarstræti 4 & 9,
P.O.B. 1131 - Reykjavik
Tel. 13133/14281/11936

INDIA - INDE
Oxford Book and Stationery Co.,
Scindia House, New Delhi 110001
Tel. 331.5896/5308
17 Park St., Calcutta 700016   Tel. 240832

INDONESIA - INDONÉSIE
Pdii-Lipi, P.O. Box 3065/JKT.Jakarta
Tel. 583467

IRELAND - IRLANDE
TDC Publishers - Library Suppliers,
12 North Frederick Street, Dublin 1
Tel. 744835-749677

ITALY - ITALIE
Libreria Commissionaria Sansoni,
Via Lamarmora 45, 50121 Firenze
Tel. 579751/584468
Via Bartolini 29, 20155 Milano   Tel. 365083
Editrice e Libreria Herder,
Piazza Montecitorio 120, 00186 Roma
Tel. 6794628
Libreria Hœpli,
Via Hœpli 5, 20121 Milano   Tel. 865446
Libreria Scientifica
Dott. Lucio de Biasio "Aeiou"
Via Meravigli 16, 20123 Milano   Tel. 807679
Libreria Lattes,
Via Garibaldi 3, 10122 Torino   Tel. 519274
La diffusione delle edizioni OCSE è inoltre
assicurata dalle migliori librerie nelle città più
importanti.

JAPAN - JAPON
OECD Publications and Information Centre,
Landic Akasaka Bldg., 2-3-4 Akasaka,
Minato-ku, Tokyo 107   Tel. 586.2016

KOREA - CORÉE
Kyobo Book Centre Co. Ltd.
P.O.Box: Kwang Hwa Moon 1658,
Seoul   Tel. (REP) 730.78.91

LEBANON - LIBAN
Documenta Scientifica/Redico,
Edison Building, Bliss St.,
P.O.B. 5641, Beirut   Tel. 354429-344425

**MALAYSIA/SINGAPORE -
MALAISIE/SINGAPOUR**
University of Malaya Co-operative Bookshop
Ltd.,
7 Lrg 51A/227A, Petaling Jaya
Malaysia   Tel. 7565000/7565425
Information Publications Pte Ltd
Pei-Fu Industrial Building,
24 New Industrial Road No. 02-06
Singapore 1953   Tel. 2831786, 2831798

NETHERLANDS - PAYS-BAS
SDU Uitgeverij
Christoffel Plantijnstraat 2
Postbus 20014
2500 EA's-Gravenhage   Tel. 070-789911
Voor bestellingen: Tel. 070-789880

NEW ZEALAND - NOUVELLE-ZÉLANDE
Government Printing Office Bookshops:
Auckland: Retail Bookshop, 25 Rutland Street,
Mail Orders, 85 Beach Road
Private Bag C.P.O.
Hamilton: Retail: Ward Street,
Mail Orders, P.O. Box 857
Wellington: Retail, Mulgrave Street, (Head
Office)
Cubacade World Trade Centre,
Mail Orders, Private Bag
Christchurch: Retail, 159 Hereford Street,
Mail Orders, Private Bag
Dunedin: Retail, Princes Street,
Mail Orders, P.O. Box 1104

NORWAY - NORVÈGE
Tanum-Karl Johan
Karl Johans gate 43, Oslo 1
PB 1177 Sentrum, 0107 Oslo 1Tel. (02) 42.93.10

PAKISTAN
Mirza Book Agency
65 Shahrah Quaid-E-Azam, Lahore 3 Tel. 66839

PHILIPPINES
I.J. Sagun Enterprises, Inc.
P.O. Box 4322 CPO Manila
Tel. 695-1946, 922-9495

PORTUGAL
Livraria Portugal,
Rua do Carmo 70-74, 1117 Lisboa Codex
Tel. 360582/3

**SINGAPORE/MALAYSIA -
SINGAPOUR/MALAISIE**
See "Malaysia/Singapor". Voir
« Malaisie/Singapour»

SPAIN - ESPAGNE
Mundi-Prensa Libros, S.A.,
Castelló 37, Apartado 1223, Madrid-28001
Tel. 431.33.99
Libreria Bosch, Ronda Universidad 11,
Barcelona 7   Tel. 317.53.08/317.53.58

SWEDEN - SUÈDE
AB CE Fritzes Kungl. Hovbokhandel,
Box 16356, S 103 27 STH,
Regeringsgatan 12,
DS Stockholm   Tel. (08) 23.89.00
Subscription Agency/Abonnements:
Wennergren-Williams AB,
Box 30004, S104 25 Stockholm Tel. (08)54.12.00

SWITZERLAND - SUISSE
OECD Publications and Information Centre,
4 Simrockstrasse,
5300 Bonn (Germany)   Tel. (0228) 21.60.45
Librairie Payot,
6 rue Grenus, 1211 Genève 11
Tel. (022) 31.89.50
United Nations Bookshop/
Librairie des Nations-Unies
Palais des Nations,
1211 - Geneva 10
Tel. 022-34-60-11 (ext. 48 72)

TAIWAN - FORMOSE
Good Faith Worldwide Int'l Co., Ltd.
9th floor, No. 118, Sec.2
Chung Hsiao E. Road
Taipei   Tel. 391.7396/391.7397

THAILAND - THAILANDE
Suksit Siam Co., Ltd.,
1715 Rama IV Rd.,
Samyam Bangkok 5   Tel. 2511630
INDEX Book Promotion & Service Ltd.
59/6 Soi Lang Suan, Ploenchit Road
Patjumamwan, Bangkok 10500
Tel. 250-1919, 252-1066

TURKEY - TURQUIE
Kültur Yayinlari Is-Türk Ltd. Sti.
Atatürk Bulvari No: 191/Kat. 21
Kavaklidere/Ankara   Tel. 25.07.60
Dolmabahce Cad. No: 29
Besiktas/Istanbul   Tel. 160.71.88

UNITED KINGDOM - ROYAUME-UNI
H.M. Stationery Office,
Postal orders only: (01)211-5656
P.O.B. 276, London SW8 5DT
Telephone orders: (01) 622.3316, or
Personal callers:
49 High Holborn, London WC1V 6HB
Branches at: Belfast, Birmingham,
Bristol, Edinburgh, Manchester

UNITED STATES - ÉTATS-UNIS
OECD Publications and Information Centre,
2001 L Street, N.W., Suite 700,
Washington, D.C. 20036 - 4095
Tel. (202) 785.6323

VENEZUELA
Libreria del Este,
Avda F. Miranda 52, Aptdo. 60337,
Edificio Galipan, Caracas 106
Tel. 951.17.05/951.23.07/951.12.97

YUGOSLAVIA - YOUGOSLAVIE
Jugoslovenska Knjiga, Knez Mihajlova 2,
P.O.B. 36, Beograd   Tel. 621.992

Orders and inquiries from countries where
Distributors have not yet been appointed should be
sent to:
OECD, Publications Service, 2, rue André-Pascal,
75775 PARIS CEDEX 16.

Les commandes provenant de pays où l'OCDE n'a
pas encore désigné de distributeur peuvent être
adressées à :
OCDE, Service des Publications. 2, rue André-
Pascal, 75775 PARIS CEDEX 16.

71602-03-1988

1980-1983:   *Competitive Carrier Rulemaking:* "Non-dominant" carriers should not be subject to rate, service or entry and exit regulations.

1981:   *Resale/Sharing* of intercity public switched phone services authorised.

1982:   *Modification of Final Judgement* resulted in divestiture of AT&T and ended antitrust action of 1974.

1986:   *Computer Inquiry III:* Structural separation requirements to be replaced by other non-structural safeguards (Comparably Efficient Interconnection, Open Network Architecture).

therefore excess capacity is the norm and where pricing policies can be important in generating traffic, a flexible interpretation of this article is required to ensure effective competition. Such an interpretation must ensure that there is sufficient capacity, in a dynamic context, to result in effective competition, as well as preventing excess capacity which may lead to excessive price competition and a potential for a dominant carrier to abuse its position.

The MPT is actively examining trends in networking among enterprises and is taking measures to promote networking. A key factor in this context is to adjust different protocols in order to enable smooth and efficient development of networks. Tax exemption systems exist for new equipment installed by Type I and general Type II carriers and small companies may obtain tax reductions when investing in some types of telecommunications equipment.

European Commission

The European Commission (EC) has over recent years become increasingly involved in telecommunications policy[23]. The Commission's Telecommunications Action Programme, approved by Council in 1984[24] set the overall policy framework for Community goals. Progress on these goals has been made through the adoption of a number of Decisions, Regulations, Directives and Recommendations which have been developed in conjunction with the Member states and which have been developed by the Council of Ministers of the EC. In following this Action Programme proposals by the Commission have emphasized the following areas:

- Co-ordinated efforts regarding future development of telecommunications in the Community and common infrastructure projects in the areas of ISDN, digital mobile communications and the introduction of future broadband communications;
- Creation of a Community-wide market for terminals and equipment and promotion of Europe-wide standards. In this context mutual recognition of type approval for telecommunications terminal equipment is being implemented in stages[25];
- Promotion of industrial co-operation in the field of pre-competitive research covering the technologies required for Integrated Broadband Communications[26]; and
- Promotion of advanced communications in the peripheral regions of the Community[27].

The Community has taken an important initiative in its recent proposals in a Green Paper for the development of a common market for telecommunications services and equipment which "aim at progressively introducing full Community-wide competition to the terminal market, and as far as possible and justified at this stage, to telecommunications services"[28].

The EC is proposing that its involvement in telecommunications service policy will be based on the provisions in the Treaty of Rome regarding, in general, the responsibility to set up a common market and ensure that obstacles to trade and competition are removed, as well as the requirement for increased harmonization of policies and, more specifically, on competition policy provisions. The March 1985 European Court of Justice decision on telex forwarding is being viewed as an important decision which may be used to bring about changes in the regulatory framework. The court ruled that government-sanctioned monopoly practices could conflict with the Treaty of Rome's Article 86 antitrust prohibitions. In an 1982 ruling, the EC argued that:

"maintenance of obsolete systems through measures taken by an undertaking in a dominant position is an abuse under Article 86*(b)* – in that it limits technical development to the prejudice of consumers"[29].

35

The EC has argued further that restrictions imposed by undertakings which are in a dominant position may be an abuse of that position, even where the dominant position has been conferred on it by authority. For example, recent EC initiatives have played a role in helping reduce the Deutsche Bundespost monopoly on modems and led it to abandon plans to extend its monopoly to cordless telephones.

Proposals in the Green Paper argue for three essential modifications:

- In the long run complete opening of the terminal equipment market to competition;
- The opening of the network under fair competitive conditions for service providers from other Community Member states;
- A clear separation of regulatory and operational functions of telecommunications administration. It is proposed that a "reserved services" monopoly be defined which would be the exclusive domain of telecommunications administrations and allow for unrestricted provision of all other services within and between Member states.

United Kingdom

The 1984 Telecommunications Act transferred ownership of British Telecom to the private sector. In November of 1984 the government sold 50.2 per cent of shares in British Telecom but remained as the largest single shareholder[30]. Unlike AT&T, but like NTT in Japan, British Telecom (BT) was sold as a complete unit with its range of subsidiary activities and with a dominant market position. The licence provisions of BT include the obligation to provide universal service and specifically service rural customers. The licence also specifies that BT price increases for the period up to 1989 must be at least 3 percentage points below the annual rate of inflation. This applies to price changes for business and residential line rentals, local calls and trunk calls taken together. Facility competition to BT is limited to Mercury which was in fact licensed before BT's privatisation. Mercury's licence gives the company full rights as a public telecommunications operator and obliges the company to build a basic network linking the major cities, but does not impose an obligation on Mercury to provide a universal service. The United Kingdom has committed not to license a further network operator[31] until at least 1990 when the position will be reviewed. The Telecommunications Act has had the effect of increasing competition in local public switched services. In the mobile radio-telecommunications sector two companies have been licenced to run competing nationwide cellular radio telecommunication networks while substantial radio frequencies have been assigned to two national and a number of regional private mobile radio networks as well as several nationwide networks.

An important feature of the Telecommunications Act was the provision for the appointment of an independent regulator, the Director General of Telecommunications, who heads the Office of Telecommunications (Oftel) which took over overseeing responsibility from the Department of Trade and Industry. One of Oftel's responsibilities is the monitoring and enforcement of licences granted by the Secretary of State for Trade and Industry to public telecommunications operators in the post-1984 regime. The conditions and provisions of licences for value-added network services are also set by the Department of Trade and Industry. Type approval procedures have also become the responsibility of an independent body – the British Approvals Board for Telecommunications who make their recommendations to OFTEL.

Prior to 1984, important changes included the separation of the Post Office from telecommunications services in 1981 – a process which has still not occurred in some countries (e.g. Germany). The British Telecom monopoly was also curtailed in 1981 with regard to freeing subscriber equipment, limiting BT to a first telephony monopoly and, by the 1981 British Telecommunications Act, allowing the licensing of competing network operators. The first telephone monopoly was abolished in 1985. Licences issued since 1984 permitted limited resale/sharing of private leased lines connected at one end to public switched networks. The resale of leased lines connected at both ends to public switched networks is prohibited until at least 1989. However, significant liberalisation has occurred in the licensing of value-added and data services.

France

In France the telecommunications monopoly is not a Constitutional monopoly and, under existing Acts, the monopoly provisions make it necessary to obtain authorisation to provide telecommunications services. The state has, therefore, not the sole de jure right to provide such services. The state can also at its discretion allow a third party to establish telecommunications services which provides government with a wide ranging freedom to alter the service structure. Flexibility in service structure has allowed the Direction Générale des Télécommunications (DGT) to set up wholly-owned subsidiary bodies operating as private companies. These companies (e.g. Transpac for packet switching) still maintain a monopoly in their respective areas.

Changes in telecommunications regulations made in recent years have been important but have not significantly improved the competitive environment or liberalised the service structure. Some of the major changes include:

- An important legal change, perhaps unique to the French PTT, is the acceptance of responsibility by the telecommunications administration in the event of gross negligence by the operator. Increasingly as OECD societies are based on information technology and on-line services, the requirement for carriers to take legal responsibility for access, security and other obligations related to the carriage of information may need to be addressed;
- Adjustments in tariff rates have been taking place over several years to readjust the ratio existing between local calls and toll calls (approximately 1:20 in France compared to 1:40 in Japan) and to bring prices closer to real costs;
- Recent initiatives by the French government have stressed the need for clearer budgetary and accounting responsibility by the telecommunications administration, in particular avoiding distorting its budget by compelling it to contribute to general government funds or for industrial policy purposes. This will relieve the DGT from direct contributions of funds to the government, involvement in financing the filière électronique programme and covering postal service losses;
- The major change affecting the telecommunications service structure in France is the creation of a Commission Nationale de la Communication et des Libertés (CNCL) which has responsibility for the oversight of the principles governing the establishment and use of telecommunications installations and the operation and use of telecommunications services. This independent regulatory agency will separate the role of service provider and regulator which had been held by the same organisation, the DGT. The CNCL will be responsible for communications irrespective of the type of transmission (satellite, cable, microwave) or content (sound, image, data, telephony). Such widespread responsibility is important given the evolution in technology and the increasing ability to integrate services over the same transmission facilities.

However, initially, changes are not expected to be rapid. Present policy is to submit a competition law relative to telecommunications only by the end of 1987 to Parliament and the initial competence of the CNCL will be limited to private networks and not public networks, and it will not have competence on VANS at present. French policy seems to favour transforming the DGT into an enterprise operating under company law (responsible for paying taxes to the State) but maintaining its monopoly except for value-added services. For such services it appears that a particular effort will be made to ensure that service providers have equal access to the basic telecommunications infrastructure.

Although the steps taken appear limited, experience has shown that their impact could be much greater than expected, depending to a large extent on the independence of the CNCL and how it interprets its role. The United States situation, for example, has shown that:

"Government and Communications regulatory authorities throughout the late sixties and seventies consistently overestimated their ability to manage or control competitive developments, and underestimated the speed with which competition would materialise, notwithstanding relatively cautious Government policies. By the middle to late seventies, the small, procompetitive steps of a few years earlier had produced major changes".[32]

Germany

Under the German Constitution, and by law, the Deutsche Bundespost (DBP) is responsible for:

"organising telecommunications, ensuring that this organisation is maintained and supplying and performing the telecommunications services required as one of the necessities of life."[33]

It has been argued that this responsibility does not explicitly require a monopoly service structure per se although it has been interpreted as requiring one. The fact that the DBP is the telecommunications carrier and regulatory body implies that it is possible for the DBP to transfer its rights and responsibilities, or part of them, to private firms[34]. Constitutional experts are, however, not in agreement, but the prevailing view is that such a transfer would be possible only to a limited extent and would not apply to the operation of public networks. The question of legal or constitutional responsibilities for the provision of telecommuhnications services and how they have to be met is an important factor in terms of structural change for many OECD countries. An alternative to a monopolistic framework for providing and ensuring that universal telecommunications services are maintained is a competitive framework, which, as long as supervisory and regulatory responsibility exists can be at least as efficient in providing universal service as a monopolistic framework and often more efficient in providing the range of telecommunications services required by various end users.

The DBP maintains regulatory authority over the network, provides services in competitive sectors and operates as a monopoly service provider without clear structural separation of these functions. In 1981 a Monopoly Commission report called for excluding the Bundespost from the equipment market (except for the 1st telephone) but recommended that it still should maintain its equipment approval authority and monopoly on transmission. The Central Telecommunications Registration Office (ZZF) was established in 1982 with the responsibility for approving terminal equipment. Recent changes have allowed liberalisation in the purchase and atachment of modems by firms – however, testing and approval procedures for modems remain with the DBP. Foreign terminal equipment manufacturers have, at times, expressed concern regarding DBP quality standards which are viewed as overly stringent relative to other countries.

The DBP has been the most criticised of the major telecommunications administrations in OECD countries[35] – it is claimed that it is bureaucratic, slow in providing new services and up-to-date technology and expensive as regards business services and in the equipment it provides. For example, the planned degree of digitalisation of the network is well below that of Germany's major trading partners within the Community (see Table II-5) and in terms of the level of modernisation of its central switching equipment (see Table IV-3). On the other hand the DBP has had one of the highest growth rates of the OECD countries in terms of telephone sets and main lines per capita since 1974, as well as the highest rate of per capita investment.

Critics of the DBP argue that it is deliberately slowing down changes in the telecommunications service framework since with an integrated services digital network it will, as the network operator, be in a position to provide a range of VAN services, particularly those with network-related features. The DBP, on the other hand, believes that it will be able to offer certain services cheaper than private firms as a result of economies of scope. The DBP is implementing a policy of tariff harmonization of switched and non-switched services, based on volume-sensitive tariff principles, in order to make it uneconomical to engage in simple resale of capacity, and to shift users to the PSTN. The DBP views the concept of usage-dependent tariffication as a means to enable it to finance its socio-political obligations without loosing market share to private firms engaged in simple resale of leased lines.

In early 1985 an official Government Commission for Telecommunications was set up to examine telecommunications strategy and the DBP. This Commission will not report until the autumn of 1987 – it is therefore unlikely that, on the basis of this report, any important structural changes will be made in the telecommunications service framework until about 1989. As in other countries (e.g. France, Switzerland) the DBP is a major employer in the country with a highly unionised work force. Opposition by the unions to changes in telecommunications service structures is expected to be a major factor in impeding change.

Other Countries

Many other OECD countries are in the process of examining or undertaking structural changes in their telecommunications service framework. Some of these are highlighted here.

In *Australia* the authorities argue that, because of the significance attached to the telecommunications infrastructure for economic and social goals the pace and form of change in regulations need to be carefully managed. Telecom Australia has recently issued a draft proposal on Value Added Services Regulations Policy which sets out to detail which services will be approved and those for which approval will be on a case by case basis and those which will not be approved[36]. The monopoly by Telecom Australia for certain equipment supply, maintenance and in particular the installation of the first telephone has been challenged recently as being in breach of the Trade Practices Act. In *Belgium* a government appointed commission made its recommendations at the end of 1986 to the Government. It recommended that the Régie des Télégraphes et des Téléphones retain its monopoly on the basic network, that regulatory and operating activities be separated and a new regulatory body be set up. The Commission also recommended that terminal equipment markets be liberalised over the next five years. In *Canada* the Canadian Radio-television and Telecommunications Commission (CRTC) allowed CNCP Telecommunications to interconnect its facilities to the local telephone networks of Bell Canada and B.C. Tel (in 1979 and 1981 respectively) for the provision of competitive data and private line voice services. In 1985 the CRTC issued a major decision adressing a number of structural and competition issues. The Commission denied an application by CNCP to compete with the telephone companies in the provision of long distance telephone services. The Commission acknowledged the potential benefits that competition would yield, particularly lower long distance rates, but denied the CNCP application on its specific merits. In the same decision the CRTC allowed the interconnection of B.C. Rail facilities to the local telephone network of B.C. Tel for the provision of competitive data and private line voice services; allowed the interconnection of private local intraexchange systems and public data local intraexchange systems to the facilities of the federally regulated carriers; and allowed the resale and sharing of carrier services except for the purpose of providing long distance telephone service. Earlier, in a 1984 decision, the CRTC formalized regulatory arrangements for the provision of enhanced services by carriers and other providers. Carriers are required to provide basic transmission services to other enhanced service providers who will not be regulated. Users may attach their own terminal equipment in federally regulated areas and most provincially regulated areas. As noted, most decisions introducing increased competition apply only in federally regulated areas. However, within the scope of the current telecommunications policy review, federal, provincial and territorial governments are consulting on the possible development of a competition policy framework that could be applied in all areas of Canada.

Apart from the liberalisation of certain types of terminal equipment the *Danish* telecommunications monopoly has remained unchanged. Denmark is preparing for liberalisation of all terminal equipment located at the subscriber's premises (at present telephone sets, telex terminals, some modems and PABXs are under the monopoly). A neutral type approval body has also been established. In *Italy* the telecommunication structure is characterised by a monopoly regime shared by four major service providers operating either under government control (long distance telephony; telex) or under company law (local and toll telephone and data; inter-continental services). A current government project envisages the consolidation of these entities into two service providers operating under company law, one for all national services and one for all international telecommunication services. Liberalisation exists for end-user terminals and value-added services connected to a public telecommunications network. The public operating companies can compete in these areas. In *New Zealand* the recent Post Office Review – still under consideration by government – recommended that telecommunications be separated from the Post Office and become a completely independent business unit. The Review recommended, however, that basic network services remain a monopoly, while customer premises be deregulated, and enhanced network services be deregulated and open to market competition. The Review however states the "a precise definition of what falls within the description of 'enhanced network' services be agreed"[37]. The *Netherlands* has decided to separate postal and telecommunications services effective in 1989 as subsidiaries of a state-owned limited liability company. PTT monopoly on equipment and VAN markets will also be opened in 1989. Regulation of telecommunications services will also come under an independent agency. The PTT will also be free to raise capital on the open market.

The role of the telecommunications administration in *Norway* is changing in that customer premises equipment is being liberalised and a neutral regulatory-type approval body established. *Spain* has recently submitted a draft law on regulation of telecommunications to Parliament which outlines the conditions of telecommunications services – basic and value-added – and introduces liberalisation for customer-premises equipment. The law also proposes the creation of an independent Consultative Council on Telecommunications. In *Sweden* the Televerket's monopoly has remained virtually unchanged, with the exception of liberalisation of certain customer premises equipment. Further liberalisation is expected by opening the market to PABXs and high speed modems. Full resale of leased-line capacity is also under consideration. *Switzerland* is in the process of redrafting its telecommunications act. While this is expected to partly liberalise equipment attachment provisions, the monopoly of the PTT is expected to remain unchanged as regards the basic telecommunications network.

3. New Service Areas and Concepts

Technological change has had important structural impacts on telecommunications networks. Transmission costs have become less distance-sensitive, costs of routing calls have declined rapidly as have the costs of switching. Since the early to mid-1970s the development and application of analogue to digital conversion techniques has successfully altered network structures. Present telecommunications networks in OECD countries can be characterized as digital islands interspersed between analogue systems. The rate of system digitalisation varies from country to country. Similarly, on the basis of current plans there will remain important differences among OECD countries in their degree of digitalisation (Table II-5). Thus, by 1990 it is planned that 90 per cent of toll switches and 100 per cent of transmission facilities will be digital in the United Kingdom whereas for Canada by 1990 it is estimated that 73 per cent of toll switching and 30 per cent of local switching will be digital. It may be expected that important regional variations will also exist within most countries as to the rate of digitalisation. However, for most countries the network development concepts are similar, involving a transition from the present digital/analogue network mix towards an integrated digital network and then an integrated services digital network (ISDN). Germany is planning to offer nationwide ISDN by 1993 in the sense that all interested customers who require a digital ISDN station will be served.

Table II-5. **Degree of digitalisation of the telephone network by 1990**

(According to current planning by the network operators)

Country	Subscribers (main lines)	Degree of digitalisation for		
		Transmission	Switching (local)	Switching (long-distance)
	(Millions)	(In percent)		
Germany	28.6	50	10	22
France	27.0	70	70	75
Italy	21.7	45	25	36
Netherlands	6.3	95	35	15
Belgium	4.0	50	29	75
Luxembourg	0.2	35	8	10
United Kingdom	20.0	100	42	90
Ireland	1.2	70	65	85
Denmark	3.0	85	23	40
Greece	4.5	15	15	25
Spain	12.2	47	5	45
Portugal	1.9	70	20	30

Source: CEPT and Commission of the European Community Studies, cited in Commission of the European Communities, Green Paper on the Development of the Common Market for Telecommunications Services and Equipment, Brussels, 26th May 1987.

Two related issues are raised from these changing technological trends concerning, in particular, the service covering of telecommunications administrations: these relate to value-added network services and the implications of ISDN.

Value Added Network Services (VANS)

The convergence of computer and telecommunications technology led to a situation where computer services were being provided on telecommunications networks, where data was being transferred and processed and where computer messaging was taking place through networks. While in an analogue telecommunications system it was possible, with some exceptions, to differentiate between a basic telecommunications service and a non-basic service, in a digital system such differentiation is becoming increasingly impossible. The need to differentiate between services is not trivial in that while traditionally basic telecommunications services were regulated, computer-related services have not been and are considered as falling in the domain of private industry.

The debate about trying to differentiate services began in 1971 when the FCC in the United States distinguished three categories of services in its Computer I decision: these were regulated telecommunications services, non-regulated data processing services and hybrid services. The latter were to be regulated on a case-by-case basis depending on whether they were viewed as being closer to telecommunications or to data processing. Subsequently in Computer II (1976) the distinction was made between "basic services" and "enhanced services". "Basic" implied the mere transport of a message from point-to-point with the message/information remaining unchanged. On the contrary an enhanced service was viewed as offering additional features or service attributes to a basic service (usually storage, code or protocal conversions). A VAN service would therefore have to offer additional features to those of normal carrier services, including message storage and processing in the network.

By implication, a VAN service was not viewed as a carriage service, and therefore could be supplied by unregulated private enterprises. In effect VANS offer additional functions to normal carrier services. In reality, however, it is difficult to determine when a particular information "package" leaves the computer and enters the network, that is, up to which point does it remain an application function and when does it become a network function. Because many functions occur in the network, many telecommunications administrations have argued that such functions are network functions, that is, linked with the transportation of the message and therefore should come under the purview of PTTs. In effect packet switching which was originally considered as as VAN service in the United States, is now considered by many telecommunications administrations as a basic service and offered on a monopoly basis.

The significant actual and potential growth in value-added services[38], and therefore revenue implications, has led may telecommunications administrations to argue that they should be responsible for providing such services, particularly when a network function is involved. Further, it is argued, that declining growth in basic services and responsibility in investing in digital networks requires that telecommunications administrations augment their revenue in order to ensure that they continue to provide universal services at a reasonable cost. However, increasingly value-added network services are viewed as an economic input in production and service industries, and for such users it is therefore highly relevant how such services are provided, the choices available and the prices charged. In this context it has been argued that given the economic importance of value-added network serving it is necessary to reconsider policies which negatively affect their development[39].

Projected growth for the market value of VAN services in Japan is for an increase from

$150 million in 1986 to $2 billion in 1995. Already Japan has 170 Type II General VANs and 8 Special Type II VANs (see footnote 19 for definitions). The European market for VANs is, according to some estimates, projected to grow from its present level of $200 million to $5 billion in 1992[40] according to some estimates, with the United Kingdom and France as the most important markets. In the United Kingdom there are over 160 companies offering nearly 690 different types of services for the manufacturing and service sectors.

The issues raised by the debate on VANS hinge around the difficulty in delineating boundaries, in a rapidly evolving technological and service matrix, between monopoly telecommunications network-based services and those which can be offered on a competitive basis. At the boundary it is particularly difficult to determine those services which have a more or less, significant level of value-added and which may be considered as falling outside, or within, a common carrier service. Such a boundary is in any case arbitrary and subject to change since service offerings which are considered specialised today may become standard in the future. It has also been argued that it is not sufficient for regulatory purposes to use technical criteria to differentiate basic services from value-added services but there may be a need to determine if a service is, or will be, universal or if its market is specific. There is also a need to determine under what conditions telecommunications administrations can operate in the value-added network service market. From the user point of view it is clearly necessary to provide a stable policy environment to allow investment planning as well as criteria which are transparent and non-discretionary.

It is in recognition of the difficulty in resolving the above issues that the Commission of the European Communities has argued that:

"A stable "natural" boundary line between a "reserved services" sector and a "competitive services" sector (including in particular "value-added services") is not possible. Due to technological development – the trend towards integration – any definition (and reservation) of a service can only be temporary and must be subject to review if it is not to impede the overall development of telecommunications services".[41]

The relative advantages and disadvantages of monopoly versus competitive supply of VANS is an issue which will continue to undergo further investigation. There may be cases where the widespread diffusion of a new service, nationally and internationally, available to all customers, requires co-ordinated action at the national level, whereas specialised requirements of the business customer can only be met through private sector initiatives. In either event, however, limited or full market entry is the best means to ensure that a service is provided efficiently and that the requirements of all users are being met.

PTT network operators argue that liberalising the provision of VAN services would result in private companies cream-skimming and thus reducing revenue of PTTs leaving only the non-profitable services under their responsibility. In the long-run it is contended that this would hurt their capability to provide basic services. There is no evidence that this would occur, rather it is more likely that efficiency in providing such services would be enhanced. In certain cases the limited entry of competitors could be envisaged to ensure that there is sufficient time for administrations to adjust to a new environment. It is also more likely that rapid growth of such services in a private, competitive environment will stimulate the use of communications in general to the benefit of the telecommunications administration[42]. Many PTTs are also concerned that competitive service providers will add minimum features to existing network functions. However, attempts to define "trivial" or "non-trivial" value-added will necessarily be arbitrary as well as a function of technological evolution. It is often argued that PTTs can ensure standardisation by controlling VAN services. Thus:

"(it is) a task of prime importance to offer ... customers – as an extra service for their benefit – telecommunications services that have largely been standardized."[43]

The basis of economic growth is the maximisation of economic opportunities which in turn depends on choice rather than constraining service providers and users to given systems, the growth of which is dependent on one-service provider's investment decisions. The standardization process can if necessary be separated from the provision of the service itself. The international movement towards open system interconnection standards overcomes this objection. In the U.K. licence conditions for large VAN providers will impose obligations to meet OSI standards.

In certain countries where private VAN services can be offered the common carrier can also provide competing services. In such situations the issue of "bottleneck monopoly" – as referred to in United States antitrust case law – may become increasingly important. This issue would arise when an integrated monopoly refuses to provide an unintegrated competitor use of the transmission monopoly so as to prevent competition in the VAN service area. The need for an adequate, and independent, regulatory body is therefore important. Such a body would also allow telecommunications administrations to compete with private suppliers under conditions of fair competition, in particular to ensure that monopoly profits from basic services are not used to subsidise VAN services.

The issue regarding the international implications of differing VAN definitions is becoming increasingly important in that they generate different market access opportunities among trading partners. In this regard, the work of the Preparatory Committee for the World Administrative Telegraph and Telephone Conference will be of relevance to the extent that the proposed new International Telecommunication Convention applies only to traditional basic services or has a wider coverage. Some countries have argued that the terms and definitions of the Convention must be limited to services offered to the public to avoid extending the coverage to value-added services. Other countries believe that telecommunications services offered internationally require a minimum number of rules defined within a legal framework and applicable to all service providers.

The fact that different countries use different definitions to delineate boundaries between basic telephone services and enhanced services could create problems at the international level in that differences in such regulations can result in unbalanced market access opportunities. There is a concern by many PTTs that liberal access by VAN services will result in important market penetration by foreign firms, but as long as restrictive access remains local, firms will be unable to obtain sufficient expertise to compete effectively. There is also a danger for countries which lag behind in adjusting regulations, that trade will occur increasingly between countries which have adjusted their structures and allow private provision of VAN services internationally to the longer-term detriment of countries which do not allow the participation of the private sector in this market.

There is also a need for adjustment in the international regulatory framework, particularly as regards CCITT Recommendation D1 "General Principles for the Lease of International Private Leased Telecommunications Circuits" where it is recommended that resale of private leased circuit capacity should not be undertaken. The CCITT has only recently started to study the VAN situation and will report in mid-to end-1987. It may therefore be several years before adjustments are made to existing recommendations. Continued strong user participation is needed in this forum to ensure that changes in recommendations do not reflect solely the telephone administrations' point of view. It can also be argued that trade policy officials should also be in a position to review recommendations in order to assess their trade implications.

The experience of the United States has shown that legal (or engineering/economic) definitions of VANS are not practical. In Canada, similar to the United States, an enhanced service is defined as any service beyond basic offering of transmission capacity for movement of information. Regulated carriers in Canada may offer VAN services but are regulated to ensure that they do not cross-subsidise. The difficulty in defining in certain cases a network service from a VAN service, has resulted in Phase 1 of Computer III in the United States, dropping the condition that a carrier had to provide enhanced services through a separate subsidiary[44]. In Japan there is no attempt to define VANs explicitly, but implicitly the definition is facilities-based rather than service-based. France uses the International Standards Organisation Open systems Interconnect model and divides services into seven classes, maintaining dominance over the three that control transmission[45]. Below this, subsidiaries of the DGT have been created to provide services although there is no de jure monopoly.

Integrated Services Digital Networks (ISDN)

ISDN is a network concept implemented through digital switching and transmission paths providing a wide range of traffic and value-added processing services, and defined on the basis of standardization of a wide range of user interfaces. The emphasis of ISDN is on standardizing network capabilities rather than services per se. The slow shift from existing separate telecommunications networks, specialized facilities and VANS to an integrated system is based on developments in digital switching and transmission which allows all information (voice, data, imagery, text) to be transmitted as binary digits, therefore in an undifferentiated form.

The decisions taken in countries with regard to the interpretation of the user/network interface standards will be important in terms of terminal market development, all access to ISDN and the allocation of "intelligence" between networks and terminal equipment. In many countries field trials are already taking place to test ISDN concepts and in some, the introduction of public ISDN services will occur over the next few years. The Council of the European Community has adopted a recommendation that:

"administrations should plan to provide by 1993 ISDN access for a number equivalent to 5 per cent of 1983 subscriber main lines. ... The territorial coverage should be sufficient to permit 80 per cent of customers to have the option of the ISDN access"[46].

Standards for ISDN have been in the process of formulation for several years by the Comité Consultatif International Télégraphique et Téléphonique of the International Telecommunication Union.

The concept of ISDN raises several key issues still under debate and which are of longer-term significance for telecommunications service structures. For example, some argue that ISDN and the integration of services will offer important economies of scope which will eliminate the need for separate network facilities for data and other services. In this context there is concern by users that the concept will be used to increase the monopoly position of PTTs and force all users onto the public switched network. In effect it may be possible to eliminate the need for dedicated networks and argue against the requirement for competing facilities. Many large users feel that they will continue to require dedicated facilities in parallel with ISDN. It has been argued that ISDN will help "the PTTs to demonstrate that they can provide their countries' users with the telecommunications services they require and hence help the PTTs resist liberalisation moves"[47]. Arguments that a single network operator is more efficient in an ISDN requirement need to be tested in a market environment.

ISDN may make it difficult to differentiate between basic and enhanced services. Many users suspect that telecommunications administrations are delaying in opening the market to certain privately-offered VAN services, in that they view such services as being offered intrinsically within an ISDN network. CCITT have divided telecommunications services into two categories; bearer services and teleservices. In effect these categories define services according to their position in the different levels of the OSI model. Bearer services have attributes classified as information transfer, access and general attributes. Teleservices provide the complete capability for communication between users of specified user terminals. Teleservices have both operational and commercial attributes. The issue of whether imagery will be offered on ISDN, and the evolution towards integrated broadband communications, is important, as is how this relates to existing market structures where cable broadcasting is offered on a private competitive basis.

It is not clear how tariff principles will change with ISDN. In particular there is concern that tariffs will be used to force users on to ISDN and that network operators may use cross-subsidisation to offer competitive services. The Groupe d'Analyse et de Prévision set up by the European Commission has suggested that tariffs on ISDN should be less distance-sensitive than at present and that tariffs for a teleservice should be the same as those for the underlying bearer service unless value is added by the network in providing the teleservice[48]. Within the framework of the European Community, it is viewed as important that tariffication principles be harmonized. On the basis of the present investment strategies of many common carriers, it would appear that the major shift from an integrated digital network to ISDN will arise from digitalising the local loop – this will also be the most burdensome step in terms of investment requirements, as well as risky in that it is not evident how residential customers will react to new services.

Other Service Areas

An important issue in structural change in telecommunications is whether the provision of new services or the reduction of costs of existing services are retarded or impeded by present regulatory conditions. In terms of new services this raises the question of whether monopoly Administrations can provide new services as quickly and as efficiently as in a liberalised environment. There is no clearcut answer to this question. There are a sufficient number of cases to illustrate that PTTs can in some cases be more efficient than the market place in stimulating a new service (examples include cellular radio, videotext, the example of telex services in Europe compared to the United States). In some cases an effective standardization process is required, in others there is a need to expand the market to a minimum threshold. Neither argument, however, implies that monopoly service provision is a necessary requirement.

NOTES AND REFERENCES

1. Data for the Regional Holding Companies in the United States for 1985 are:

	Main lines (millions)	Revenue: ($ billion)
Ameritech	14.6	9.0
Bell Atlantic	15.1	9.1
Bellsouth	14.5	10.7
NYNEX	13.6	10.3
Pacific Telesis	11.7	8.5
US West	11.2	7.8
Southwestern Bell	11.0	7.9

2. Increased liberalisation in allowing the purchase of telephone sets (in some countries this includes the first set) and falling prices of sets has resulted in a considerable boom in installation by households of two or more sets. This implies that the use of telephone sets per capita as an indicator of telephone penetration rates is rapidly becoming invalid.

3. Differences in real GDP per capita may explain differences in penetration rates between the highly industrialized OECD countries and the less industrialized Member countries, but do not explain differences between countries which have similar levels of GDP per capita.

4. Up to the end of 1983 AT&T was still the dominant carrier in the United States with a monopoly in telecommunications services except in long-distance where it nevertheless still had a de facto dominant position with 80 per cent of the market in 1986.

5. It is difficult to make such efficiency comparisons, especially between PTTs and private companies. Differences in line maintenance services and in subcontracting procedures, diversity in service coverage, existence of operators, etc., bias comparisons especially when using employees per line.

6. Revenue per employee, in 1985, for four of the Bell Operating Companies in the United States (Ameritech, Bell Atlantic, GTE, NYNEX) ranged between $96 900 to $ 120 500 but this relative differential is not necessarily reflected in higher operating income per main line. This in turn, partly reflects the difficulties noted in footnote 5 above in making comparisons.

7. Studies have found that a shift to measured service charges away from flat rates has reduced call rates. For example, Jenkins and Wilkinson (in G.M. Jenkins and G. McLeod (editors), Case Studies in Time Series Analysis, Time Series Library, 1982) found that such a shift led in one region in the United States to a decrease in usage in the region of 11.8 per cent.

8. In the United Kingdom, for example, it is estimated that residential lines are used for outgoing calls for 40 minutes per week and business lines approach 4 hours per week.

9. FCC CC Docket No. 78.72 August 6th 1982, Comments of the Bell System Operating Companies and the American Telephone and Telegraph Company in Response to the Fourth Supplemental Notice of Inquiry and Proposed Rule Making.

10. Historically, telephone charges in most countries have been constrained to rates below the increase in the consumer price index. It should be noted that some rate changes may not be sufficiently well reflected in price indices. For example, recent changes in local rates in France have reduced the *price* of a local call but reduced significantly the applicable *time period* to which such a rate is applied.

11. Telecommunications Reports Vo. 53 February 11, 1987, cites estimates that 40 percent of the world's international traffic either originates or terminates in Manhattan.

12. La Tribune de l'Economie of 28th April 1986. The PTT also funds the CNES budget in the amount of FF 3.3 billion in 1985 and FF 4.3 billion in 1986.

13. OECD data exclude Denmark and Turkey, EEC excludes Denmark.

14. T. Nousaine and S. Brant "A case for capital investment", Telephony, February 2, 1987, provide estimates indicating that in 1975 100 employees were required for 10,000 access lines compared to 50 employees in 1985. Studies in countries, such as the United Kingdom, indicate a continued requirement for significant labour shedding by telecommunications service providers.

15. A complete review of changes in Member country national policies is provided in: OECD, Trends of Change in Telecommunication Policy, ICCP Series No. 13, 1987.

16. The literature tends to use deregulation and liberalisation synonymously. The latter term is preferred here given that liberalisation may have to be accompanied by new and changed regulatory frameworks.

17. United States firms had a clear technological lead in VAN technology and know-how and, therefore, given difficulties in penetrating the Japanese market in other sectors, early market entry was viewed as essential in this case. The fact that the VAN service industry is software-driven, may also have accounted for MITI's wish to stimulate the VAN market given Japan's relative weakness in software development.

18. H. Janisch and Y. Kurisaki, Reform of telecommunications regulation in Japan and Canada, Telecommunications Policy, March 1985, p. 34.

19. A Special Type II telecommunications business is one that provides large-scale telecommunications facilities to a large number of unspecified persons, or that provide telecommunications facilities between Japan and a foreign country; any other business is a General Type II. Restrictions on utilisation of leased lines were also lifted.

20. NTT shares were floated on the market starting in late 1986 and about 50 per cent of its shares will be sold between 1986-91. The government is obliged to retain one-third ownership and foreigners will not be allowed to purchase shares.

21. This includes the first telephone set.

22. As cited and translated in Japan Computer Quarterly, The Liberalisation of Telecommunications, July 1985.

23. An early effort by the European Community in implementing the decision in 1975 to improve access to scientific and technical information was aimed at developing within the community a network to facilitate direct access to information (referred to as EURONET).

24. Communication by the Commission to Council on Telecommunications, COM(84)277, 18.5.1984 and Minutes of the 979th Meeting of the Council, 17.12.1984.

25. The Council Directive of 24 July, 1986 on the initial stage of the recognition of type approval for telecommunications terminal equipment (86/361/EEC) came into force in July 1987. The Directive gives the Commission the mandate, inter alia, to designate a list of international standards and technical specifications in telecommunications to be harmonized and to request the CEPT (the European Conference of Posts and Telecommunications Administrations) to draw up common conformity specifications in the form of European Telecommunications Specifications [NETs - Normes Européennes de Télécommunications].

26. The RACE programme [Research on Advanced Communication Technology in Europe] has completed a definition phase. The Commission proposal for the main RACE programme was tabled in October 1986 and proposes expenditure of 800 million ECU over 1987-1991.

27. The Special Telecommunications Actions for Regional Development [STAR] has an allocation of 780 million ECU up to 1990.

28. Commission of the European Communities, Draft Green Paper on the Development of the Common Market for Telecommunications Services and Equipment, 26 May 1987, p. 21.

29. Common Market Report 10.443, 1982.

30. Foreign investors bought 13.7 per cent of the shares. The government may review, in April 1988, whether its shareholdings will be maintained. The government is committed not to use its rights as an ordinary shareholder to intervene in company decisions although it has the power to do so.

31. Cable television companies have been given public telecommunications operator status and an exclusive right to offer a full range of telecommunications services within a prescribed area. The U.K. has also two competing cellular mobile radio operations.

32. National Telecommunications and Information Administration, U.S. Department of Commerce, NTIA Competition Benefits Report, 8th November 1985, p. 7.

33. Submission to ICCP Second Special Session on Telecommunications by the Federal Republic of Germany in OECD, ICCP Series No. 13, op. cit.

34. This point has been argued, for example, in Neumann, K.-H., Economic Policy Toward Telecommunications, Information and the Media in West Germany, Diskussionsbeiträge zur Telekommunikationsforschung Nr.8, Juni 1984, Deutsche Bundespost, Wissenschaftliches Institut für Kommunikationsdienste.

35. See, for example, the Annual Report of the "Wise Men" to the Federal Government, 1985; the report to the Federal Government on deregulation in 1986 by the Kiel Economics Institute. A recent study by McKinsey Consultants for the Government Commission for Telecommunications (Witte Commission) argues that innovation in telecommunications is behind in Germany vis-a-vis its major trading partners, as is the introduction of certain telecommunications services. The Federation of Germany Industries (BDI) has recently echoed these comments as has the Association of German Chambers of Commerce.

36. The Australian Information Industry Association has criticised the fact that Telecom Australia is taking up the role of strategic policy maker rather than the Government.

37. Post Office Review, Report dated 21st February 1986, R.N. Mason and M.S. Morris. Experience has shown – see section following – that attempts at definitions can be fruitless.

38. Such growth is illustrated by packet switching in France:

Number of subscribers (TRANSPAC)				Number of megabits per day per subscriber		
1979	1980	1984	1985	1980	1984	1985
641	2 395	21 652	31 410	1.4	4.1	5.1*

Source: DGT
* Includes the videotex service.

39. C.C.von Weizsaecker, The Economics of Value Added Network Services, Cologne, June 1987.

40. Logica estimates. Market estimates vary considerably because of differences in defining VANS.

41. Commission of the European Communities, Green Paper, op.cit. page 219.

42. Weizsaecker, op. cit. argues (p. 10): "In a dynamic environment it is more important that competition is a social mechanism by which innovations are stimulated. The competitive process can be seen as a never ending series of experiments which try out better problem-solutions compared to those which have been available in the past. Markets characterized by monopoly are

not able to perform similar experiments. It is therefore likely that competitive markets lead to greater progress than monopoly markets".

43. *The Deutsche Bundespost's response to the telecommunications requirements of tomorrow*, The Federal Ministry of Posts and Telecommunications, Bonn, 1984, p. 5

44. The requirement is dropped *if* there is sufficient competition in the region. This condition raises other complex definitional issues.

45. These classes are Application, Presentation, Session, Transport, Network, Data Link and Physical. The last three constitute the communication subnet boundary.

46. Official Journal of the Europeen Communities 31.12.86; Recommendation L382/36.

47. Kee, R. and Lewin, D., ISDN, The Commercial Benefits, Ovum Ltd., 1986.

48. See ibid., p. 300.

Chapter III

MAIN ISSUES IN STRUCTURAL CHANGE

The previous chapter examined structural changes in the telecommunications service sector. As noted, significant changes have already taken place in several Member countries in the service sector although the rationale for such changes has not been homogeneous across countries. Substantial pressures exist in those countries where change has not occurred or where it has occurred at too slow a pace.

A large number of important issues face the main actors in the telecommunications service industry, and in particular, government policy-makers. Some of the key issues are examined in this chapter. It is important to recall, however, that it is difficult to predict the impact and outcome of technological and regulatory changes which have taken place and which will continue to affect the industry. Policy will have to adjust to take into account unforeseen impacts. On the other hand the need to take policy initiatives and adjust outdated regulatory frameworks is urgently required in several OECD countries – hesitation will only lead to increased economic costs.

1. The Basis for Intervention in Telecommunications Service Markets

Several basic arguments are usually put forward in support of the provision of telecommunications services through monopoly structures and the continued regulatory framework. In many cases little academic or other consensus has been reached as to the validity of arguments. In other cases where changes have been made to telecommunications structures they have often been based on wider economic and political considerations without explicit reference to theoretical models (although an implicit rejection of such models can be assumed).

Over the last decade a substantial economic literature has emerged arguing for or against competition in telecommunications with reference mainly to concepts of natural monopoly, sustainability of monopoly and economies of scope[1]. Closely linked to these arguments are questions of tariff structures.

The justification for the continuation of monopoly supply structures in telecommunications is usually based on the argument that telecommunications services have 'natural monopoly' characteristics[2], there are economies of scale in supply[3] and in a multiproduct industry such as telecommunications, the monopolist may have cost complementarities which lead to economies of scope. The natural monopoly may be sustainable in the sense that rival firms cannot enter profitably, or unsustainable, in that sufficient incentives exist to allow firms to enter and profitably provide some product lines despite the fact that the monopolist could produce the entire output at a lower cost than these firms.

51

The implication of the existence of a natural monopoly is that competitive entry would lead to inefficiency and consumer welfare loss. It is also argued that economies of scope exist in that joint production of the industry's output is cheaper than separate production (for example, local and toll services) at all levels of the output range.

Extensive analytical work has been undertaken to examine the empirical validity of the above concepts as they relate to telecommunications services[4]. In general the outcome of this work is inconclusive and contradictory. The lack of adequate and consistent cost data is an important constraint in this context. There is also considerable scepticism as to the validity of undertaking empirical tests, valid in a static framework and for a given vector of production characteristics and technology, and in an industry subject to rapid technological change such as experienced in telecommunications. In particular, it is often questioned to what extent such tests would be useful in formulating policy given an industry where a range of technologies exist to provide a given service mix, where new technologies and new service characteristics are emerging rapidly and where cost and demand structures are also changing rapidly.

Structural changes in the United States, the United Kingdom and Japan have implicitly rejected the use of the natural monopoly concept as a defence of monopoly supply. In the first two cases, for long-distance services and in the case of Japan, in general. Questions regarding the existence of natural monopoly were not at the forefront of arguments for change in the case of British Telecom and NTT. Rather, emphasis was placed on the need to improve management efficiency, innovative ability and service flexibility.

There is general agreement, that as a result of rapid technological change in switching and network facilities, as well as the emergence of alternative transmission technologies (microwave, satellite, cellular radio, fibre optics) that any natural monopoly characteristics which may have existed would have been significantly eroded. The move towards ISDN and integrated broadband communications may, according to some analysts change this trend, in particular as a result of strong economies of scale in the networks. There is also some general agreement that for non-basic telecommunications services natural monopoly characteristics do not exist or are not strong. This is also the case as regards terminal equipment where provision by PTTs of such equipment has been in some cases justified on the basis of economies-of-scope arguments. This would also apply to a range of value-added network services – where other arguments are usually put forward to retain monopoly control.

Arguments have been put forward that, irrespective of natural monopoly considerations, ease of entry and exit, or the threat of entry, by competing firms will discipline the monopolist to implement cost-based pricing, therefore limiting the use of predatory pricing techniques, stimulating innovation and management efficiency[5]. Market contestability can therefore replace direct regulation as a policy and reduce any potentially adverse monopoly practices. The efficiency of such a policy has been strongly questioned[6].

Other arguments given to support monopoly provision of telecommunications services include the question of external economies, the requirement to provide such services on the basis of public service considerations and the importance of the telecommunications industry to national security and in terms of industrial policy considerations. Such requirements have not been shown as being in themselves sufficient to justify any particular form of market structure.

Externalities exist when private and social costs diverge. In telecommunications, the network effect, whereby each new network subscriber enhances the value of the network for existing subscribers, is often cited as an important externality. Arguments that INTELSAT's averaged pricing structure led to externalities have been put forward[7]. Videotex may also provide an example. In the United States, the videotex market has been plagued by differing standards, geographic compartmentalisation and, as a result, a slow rate of take-up by consumers. In France on the other hand, there has been a rapid build-up in the videotex system. The transformation of directory information into an electronic form, and the free distribution to households of terminals (estimated to reach close to 2 million sets at the end of 1986) stimulated the market which was based on a unique nationwide standard. However, the cost of this form of market development has not been adequately investigated. In general terms, non-market decisions may lead to bad equipment choice and system definitions, whereas market driven development may result in insufficient scale and integration among potential customers to ensure profitability.

There is insufficient evidence that arguments based on external economies in themselves justify a monopoly service structure. Cases where successful co-ordinated market development led to efficient services on a widespread basis (cellular mobile radio in the Nordic region and teletext in Europe) were based on early standards agreement and equipment and service definitions and did not require monopoly service structures per se.

The desire to meet well-stated social policy objectives does not preclude the competitive supply of telecommunications services nor does it provide sufficient grounds for public ownership. Regulatory measures are required irrespective of market structures to ensure that users are protected from practices and results arising from unfair exercise of monopoly position, from the imperfect operation of competitive markets or from the need to adjust the outcome of different market structures to meet social goals.

Many countries, particularly the smaller economies, view the potential loss of control of the telecommunications infrastructure which could arise from allowing facilities competition and foreign entry, as a real threat. Allowing a competitive service structure would, it is believed, inevitably lead to pressure for foreign entry in service and facilities provision and therefore weaken national sovereignty. There is a need for countries to determine how perceived competing objectives, such as more liberalised market structures can be balanced against national security considerations.

There is increasing awareness that the issue of intervention and regulation in telecommunications markets is not simply based on the choice between ideal market solutions – that is on the one hand where the market is viewed as the most efficient means to allocate resources and stimulate innovation or on the other hand where a monopoly situation is preferable on the grounds that the market is unable to satisfy service requirements efficiently. Rather than ideal models, the imperatives of imperfect markets, dynamic structures and social and political realities, suggest the emergence of market structures which balance competing social and economic objectives and will reflect characteristics of the two ideal structures. A lack of a balanced approach may result in one group of users being favoured at the expense of others.

2.   Competition, Tariff Structures and Industry Adjustment

The issue of competition in telecommunications services is highly complex involving more than the resolution of theoretical arguments. The issue is not simply whether there should be competition or not, but where should it be allowed to take place, to what extent and what are the spill-over effects. The full long-term effects of competition in telecommunications services – or even of long-distance services – are not evident and are intricately linked with questions of tariff structures, social equity goals and social goals such as universal services. Some governments in favour of competition, view the adjustment to a competitive telecommunications environment as a longer-term process requiring flexibility and less radical changes than have occurred in the United States or Japan.

The basic question in the debate on monopoly versus competition in the provision of telecommunications services concerns the expected potential net benefits which can be derived from competition. The benefits are often difficult to evaluate, the costs appear more immediate and much clearer. The difficulty in evaluating benefits is that they rest on more general economic concepts: improved resource allocation, productivity, innovation, enhanced consumer choice, a lower regulatory burden and costs involved in overcoming these regulations. In short, the benefits are those attained from market competition as the most efficient tool for resource allocation – a principle accepted by all Member countries nuanced where necessary by regulation to improve allocative efficiency.

Despite these general assertions little concrete analysis is available to determine the impact of structural changes in telecommunication or the costs incurred from the existing structure. The difficulty in undertaking such analysis is based on rapidly changing technology and the difficulty in predicting developments in more liberalised market structures. On the other hand, little concrete evidence exists to indicate that, at present levels of network development, existing structures are optimal. Most telecommunications administrations, while stressing the strategic importance of telecommunications, contradict this argument by not allowing a minimum of free rein to the market in order to develop and stimulate the industry (service and equipment), give correct price signals to users for future investment decision and maximise the global benefits of this industry.

However, most OECD countries recognise that there are areas of telecommunication service provision that may benefit from competition. Controversy surrounds the methods of handling the transition from monopoly service provision to competition in the supply of public switched network and leased line services.

The concept of competition in telecommunications services is clouded by the rate structures which exist in most countries. Despite the absence of empirical evidence as to the flow of subsidies embedded in PTT rate structures, it widely is believed that high long-distance rates cross-subsidise local service rates creating a strong uneconomic incentive for competitive entry in long-distance markets. For example, in West Germany telephone tariffs are said to include subsidies resulting from rate-averaging practices. "Local calls are subsidised by long-distance calls. Rural access is subsidised by urban access. Moreover, the postal service is subsidised by telephone tariffs, which adds an additional equity component"[8]. The nature and direction of many of the subsidies in existing rate structures and the incentives they may create for competition are not well documented by empirical evidence as discussed below.

In most European countries the PTTs have claimed that rate structures are not entirely cost based, reflecting other factors such as the value of the service provided and the social utility of the service. But rate restructuring proposals designed to eliminate or reduce subsidies have not been accompanied by data that would clarify the underlying cost/price relationships among different services. In Canada, for example, Bell Canada claims that it costs $1.93 per $1.00 of revenue to provide local service, whereas the cost of long distance service is $0.32 per $1.00 of revenue. Bell and other carriers assign the total costs of access in the local cost figure. Bell Canada's (non-competitive) Local Service Revenues were $1.4 billion in 1983. Local usage costs were $0.8 billion, resulting in a contribution to access costs by the local service category of $0.6 billion. If one compares total (non-competitive) local and long distance revenues with costs excluding access, the contribution by both monopoly services amounts to $1.9 billion[9].

In Europe, where, with the exception of the United Kingdom, monopoly service provision still exists, the spill-over of United States and United Kingdom competition has created pressures to reduce long-distance rates. For example, France recently reduced prices to the

United States by 21 per cent for long-distance telephone services. Such pressure will continue and may accelerate – ensured in particular by the ability of large users to divert transatlantic traffic within Europe to profit from the cheapest routes. A similar process has already occurred in Canada where long-distance rates declined as a result of traffic diversion from the West Coast of Canada via the United States for Eastern destinations[10].

For several years countries have been restructuring rates as a result of several factors such as the need to stimulate traffic and ensure optimal use of networks and equipment, and as a result of technological change which has altered costs, in particular the sensitivity of costs to distance. In some countries, such as France, the introduction of value-added tax in telecommunications will diminish the costs of communications for firms. The above factors continue to play a role in rate restructuring. As well, the pressure for European countries to reduce long-distance rates arises from the approaches to rate restructuring that have been adopted in the United States and elsewhere where competition had already been introduced. In the United States, these pressures accompanied divestiture and changing regulation in the wake of the Modification of Final Judgment (MFJ) in 1984. The new post-divestiture competitive environment has, and is continuing to have, profound structural changes: company structures have required changing, significant readjustments in tariffs have occured, the regulatory process has become more complex and detailed[11], new accounting procedures have been required and the creation of separate accounting entitites to ensure that competitive services and non-competitive services are treated separately. As competition in long-distance markets began to push prices down in the United States, the MFJ envisaged that the contribution by long-distance revenues to local service costs would be replaced by carrier access charges. It became evident fairly quickly that largeusers of long-distance services were capable of by-passing switched networks. The FCC decided to implement, as an alternative, a per-line monthly access charge on business and residential customers[12], recognising that the customer access charge would have to be set at a level which would not induce by-pass of the local switched networks operated by the Bell Operating Companies.

The question of whether local services should be open to competition has only recently been raised as an issue in telecommunications, although similar pricing structure problems which exist, or existed, between long-distance and local services can be found in the local service framework. These involve the use of system-wide average pricing and therefore the potential for cross-subsidy which may exist between high density service areas and low density areas, and technologies which may provide incentives for by-pass[13] of the local service network. The previous Chairman of the Federal Communications Commission in the United States has suggested that complete deregulation of local telephone services and elimination of local subsidies over a three year experimental period could be envisaged[14].

For most telecommunications administrations local service has characteristics of a natural monopoly, and since it is viewed as the mainstay of universal service the question of allowing competition in local service is seldom considered. Rather, the main policy question facing telephone administrations is to what extent is it possible to allow competition in the provision of non-basic long-distance and other telecommunications services without jeopardising the goal of universal service.

The backbone of the universal sevice concept is that basic telecommunications services should be available *at a reasonable cost* to the majority of the population. It is evidently difficult to define what consitutes 'reasonable cost' : obviously historical prices paid by consumers will influence their perception of what is reasonable. It is worth noting that electricity, generally viewed on the same basis as telephony as a universal service was nonetheless subject to considerable rate increases as a result of the two oil shocks in the 1970s.

The cost of other necessary commodities has in the United States – and most OECD countries – risen at much higher rates than telecommunications services[15].

Indexes for selected commodities, United States
(1967 = 100)

Commodity	Index (March 1985)
Housing	344.7
Fuel and other utilities	388.2
Electricity	354.2
Food	309.2
Medical care	395.3
Telephone services	191.3

Source: NTIA Benefits Report, 1985.

Differences in perception as to what constitutes "reasonable" exist between North America where local telephone service flat rate pricing has been used to a large extent, in contrast to Europe where usage-based pricing has been the norm.

Two exceptions to potential local service competition should be mentioned. The first is the Illinois Universal Telephone Service Protection Law (1985)[16] which envisages phased-in competition in the intermarket service areas and local exchange markets. The law allows service providers to receive a certificate of inter-exchange service authority (beginning 1st January 1987) or local exchange service authority (beginning 1st January 1989). Applicants in the latter case must show that they will not adversely affect prices and network designs or the financial viability of the principal local exchange service provider. The threat of potential entry may be in itself sufficient to ensure that the principal service provider remains efficient and provides a service at minimum cost.

The second exception is in Japan where liberalisation has not attempted to distinguish between types of services and already several local electrical utilities are intending to offer basic services. However, since NTT is still mandated to ensure universal service, it is still unclear what authority it can wield to reduce any impact on its customer base.

In addition to cost issues, the difficulty in defining effectively a local calling zone needs to be recognised. Increasingly, technology has made telephone calls less sensitive to distance; a factor reflected in expanding local area charge zones. With fibre-optic transmission and digital networks, network usage is significantly more distance-insensitive. It needs to be recalled that there already exist large discrepancies within and between countries in local service areas. This again raises the issue of trying to segment toll and local markets. Tariffication changes in some countries, such as Norway, will be based on eliminating distance as a parameter in domestic tariffication.

There is a controversy as to whether resource misallocation has been induced in North America where basic telephone service is usually priced on a flat rate basis rather than on a per call or per unit basis. The adoption of alternative pricing structures on grounds of a more efficient pricing policy is having, and will continue to have, implications for consumer telephone charges. In many cases it is argued that the increases in these charges should be viewed positively in terms of strict economic efficiency.

It can be argued that the process of competition as introduced in the United States has, since 1959, with the *Above 890* Decision and other decisions since then, increased the adjustment burden and made adjustment more difficult[17]. This is because decisions focused exclusively on long-distance competition, rather than on the structure of the telecommunications service market as a whole, or on the fact that major changes in the pricing regime would be implemented.

The impact of competition in long-distance markets in OECD countries and changes in rate structures may lead to debate over the appropriate methods of allocating the costs of access within PTT networks. The alternatives have been widely debated in the United States and continue to be reflected in the FCC's policy of recovering access costs through end-user customer access charges. The resolution to cost allocation and rate structure problems in the telecommunications industry continues to be debated[18].

The experience in all countries which have introduced more competitive structors in telecommunications or who are moving towards more competition has been that local service prices have increased and long distance (domestic and international) have declined. The primary rationale for this is the argument that because of the social policy considerations of universal service, the pricing structure has led to long distance subsidising universal service. Competition leads to cost-based pricing requiring adjustments in the pricing structure. Fundamental differences exist among analysts pertaining to whether long-distance "subsidises" local loop costs or, since such costs are joint, the present division of costs between local service and long-distance is the correct policy and cannot be construed as a subsidy. Thus it has been argued that the "indeterminate nature of joint cost allocation and analysis prevents us from knowing with certainty whether, under the present allocation of NTS (non-traffic sensitive) costs, long-distance is subsidising local, local is subsidising long-distance, or whether each service is being assessed its proper portion of loop costs"[19]. It has not been sufficiently recognised by policy-makers that there is a need to distinguish between local services per se and local exchange facilities which supply local, long-distance and other specialised services, and that therefore there are important common costs[20]. This issue is highly relevant to current discussions in the United States regarding by-pass services. Arguments have been put forward that:

"... while by-pass services are a reality, they do not appear to be a threat to the continued viability of traditional telecommunications carriers. Ironically, the greatest threat is created by long-distance carriers and their large business customers' reluctance to pay a reasonable share of the costs they cause to be incurred for services they use."[21]

However, it should also be clear that even in a completely competitive environment for telecommunications facilities where prices reflect costs, by-pass will remain attractive to large network users because of other benefits (security, custom services, preference to internalise costs, etc.) Already, in the United States many large corporations are setting up networks and many local government bodies, State administrations and the Federal Government itself will by-pass the local switched networks. These users often account for a large percentage of revenues for established networks. Innovations to attract or maintain large users by the regional Bell Operating Companies includes offering negotiated service "packages", improving Centrex capabilities and investment in networks by carriers which by-pass their own embedded base.

European PTTs are in some cases learning from the United States' experience in deregulation. For example, recent French initiatives which will reduce long-distance and increase local service costs will, in effect, reduce the incentive for carrier competition even if allowed. Telephone administration arguments that they are required to maintain control of profitable services in order to generate revenues to contribute to local exchange plant costs will become much weaker once sufficient adjustments are made in local service tariff structures. But, underlying telephone administration arguments, is the implicit assumption that basic services cannot be provided efficiently at acceptable prices – an argument which has not been demonstrated effectively. For example, one has only to examine the efficiency of some smaller operating areas, such as Hull (UK) to counter these arguments.

Returning to the question of the threat to universal telecommunications services, and in particular the United States experience, some comments can be made:

- The argument that deregulation will jeopardise the universal service concept has no basis in that liberalisation and total unrestrained competition are different. Any danger of residential subscribers dropping-off the system can, if necessary, be compensated by direct and more transparent subsidies as for other social objectives;
- Already since divestiture telephone service charges have risen significantly in percentage terms in the United States[22]:

Average per month charges

	1983	1985	Percentage change
Flat-rate service	$10.55	$14.29	35
Measured service	$ 5.15	$ 7.81	52

Source: Consumer Federation of America.

These rate increases must be placed in the context of the longer-term trends in the real cost of telephone service which has been declining in the United States.

In the European context the prices still appear reasonable but adjustment problems for lower income consumers occurred particularly as a result of the rapidity in the changes. It should be noted that, for example, in France, when telephone rates increased 25 per cent mainly for general government revenue purposes (in 1984), there was little outcry or concern expressed as to the impact on universal service, nor any significant long-term slowdown in traffic growth. The imposition of measured time units per call (first, for every 20 minutes in 1985 reduced to 6 minutes for peak hours by 1987) has been accepted, as well, as necessary in order to institute an efficient pricing policy.

- In response to the fear that consumers would be forced to drop-off the system the FCC adopted recommendations regarding "lifeline assistance measures" to help low-income households which may be implemented by the States (approximately 13 States had or were in the process of implementing lifeline discount telephone programmes by mid-1986). Recent United States Bureau of Census data indicate that the number of households with a telephone has increased slightly between March 1984 to March 1986[23], evidence, according to the FCC that divestiture has not led to subscribers dropping-off the system[24]. However, full price-effects have still not worked their way completely through the system over this period;
- In terms of impact of deregulation it is clear that in all countries the most immediate impact will be to shift the burden of rate adjustment on to residential consumers. There are unlikely to be spill-over benefits from large users onto residential consumers, except in a very indirect way, and perhaps imperceptible to the latter. This is not however an argument against liberalisation of service provision;
- The decline in long-distance charges will benefit some residential users. It is usually assumed on the basis of existing patterns of use, that low income users will not benefit, whereas medium-to-high income consumers will benefit. Nevertheless, one can assume that changes in the relative pattern of use by different income groups may arise over time in response to price changes. In some cases, as in Japan, lower long-distance charges may be limited to heavy traffic regions.

There is need for more balance in arguments used by proponents and opponents of telecommunications service liberalisation. Thus it should be recognised that existing service rate structures in some OECD countries are becoming less viable in the face of rate restructuring in other OECD countries. It is, however, difficult to try to compare present costs and benefits with those that may result from liberalisation. Proponents of competition and economic efficiency need to recognise that cross-subsidisation may need to remain, for example, between rural and urban subscribers. There is a need by supporters of liberalisation also, to consider to what extent rate restructuring proposals work mainly to the advantage of large network users – users who may be able to better bear costs than small network users. Accepting universal service as a social goal requires that serious consideration to be given as to how to maintain this goal financially in a competitive environment – it is insufficient in this case to simply make reference to "market forces" as the final arbitrator.

But it is also necessary not to abuse the universal service argument using it not only to maintain monopoly structures but to extend them as well.

Technological changes can also be expected to play an important role in reducing the cost of providing basic local services especially in remote areas – the use of low cost satellite dish receivers, radio-based local distribution systems and cellular radio systems will be able to sevice rural customers more effectively in the future.

An important issue in the adjustment of the telecommunications service industry in some countries concerns the question of subsidies from PTT telecommunications service revenues to postal services and, in some cases, general government revenues. Increasingly the services offered by telecommunications are competitive with traditional postal services (electronic messaging, teletext) and present technological trends may lead to further reduction in areas where postal volume is important. For example, business invoicing, ordering and payment as well as document exchanges. Continued existence of the two services under the same administrative structure can lead to conflict of interest between services and may restrict innovative capacity in telecommunications (as well as in postal services). The requirement imposed on many telecommunications administrations to cover postal service losses, deprives the former of important investment resources. Rate structures that include subsidies of this nature may increase pressures for uneconomic entry and lead to a misallocation of resources within the telecommunications services industry.

3. Some Adjustment Experiences

In the United States, divestiture and deregulation of competitive service offerings of the dominant carriers has resulted in a variety of other areas of adjustment. The diverstiture requirement that equal access provisions should be made available to competitive carriers placed Other Common Carriers in a price-cost squeeze given declining long-distance charges and the fact that they lost the local connection discount they had received for lower quality connections. Ironically, this has forced the OCCs to complain that the pace of deregulation is too fast and that given AT&T's inherent advantage that the deregulaton process should slow down. To some extent this reflects the competitive process which has occurred in deregulation in the United States where emphasis has been given to loosening regulations and "freeing" the market. Given moves away from pricing on the basis of system-wide averaging, and increases in charges placed on local service customers, questions of the threat to universal services have arisen. No emphasis was given, however, to trying to obtain a more equitable market share distribution and to encouraging the market entry process. Despite some form of long-distance competition in the United States for over a decade, AT&T still maintains a dominant market share.

The question needs posing whether the logic of deregulation as well as the need to eliminate effective barriers to competition, should not allow the Bell Operating Companies to enter long-distance markets. The insistence in discriminating between markets and segmenting markets may in the longer run lead to further structural problems, much as occurred as a result of declining revenue contributions from long-distance to local service. The review slated three years after divestiture of AT&T by the MFJ (i.e. in 1987) could in this regard have important implications.

With regard to ownership, a clear distinction must be made between liberalisation and privatisation. Market structure and the implementation of effective competition is more relevant than questions of ownership of the telecommunications service provider. In this context privatising an existing service company, leaving intact its existing service base, may have beneficial impacts on managerial efficiency and company innovation[25] but does not lead to effective competition per se and may require adequate regulatory oversight to ensure that there is no abuse of dominant position; for example, in the United Kingdom, the privatisation of British Telecom was not aimed at furthering liberalisation – other measures were instituted to implement this goal. In this regard, it has been argued that government policy has overemphasized privatisation as a goal in itself when competition should have been the goal[26].

To some extent it could be argued that structural changes in the service framework in Japan are more effective and further reaching than divestiture in the United States. The concept of discrimination according to service market does not exist and regulations are fewer and simplified.

The impetus given by telecommunications service liberalisation to investment and service activity, is evident from the experience in the United States and Japan. In the United States approximately 400 companies are involved in marketing long-distance services (i.e. resellers purchasing bulk communications capacity). In Japan, at least six groups have obtained permission as Type 1 carriers and are planning to construct and operate their own telecommunications system for long-distance leased circuit services and long-distance public-switched telephone services. Significant activity has, as previously noted, been generated in the value-added network service area.

There are of course negative aspects associated with liberalisation of service structures. These may include higher local rates, and initially in the United States, customer confusion and inconvenience. Opponents of liberalisation have used these factors as proof of a net negative impact of deregulation. Rather, these factors should be viewed in terms of short-term transition costs of changing market structures.

An issue raised as a longer-term factor is also the extent to which liberalisation is turning the focus of service suppliers away from long-term network planning toward profit sensitivity and focussing efforts in lucrative service areas. This could adversely affect high-cost, low-profitability services (such as basic local service) if there is no mandated responsibility. However, there is, almost universally, such a requirement attached to the operators licence, which, with an adequate regulatory agency should provide sufficient protection. In many cases, this type of protection even surpasses existing instruments available to ensure that the operator is fulfilling the required mandate.

4. **The International Framework**

The structural changes which have taken place in telecommunications services in several Member countries have important longer-term international implications. Prior to the early

1980s, the national telecommunications service structures were similar in market structure, and telecommunications policy was viewed primarily in terms of its domestic implications. Since then, different market structures have changed perceptions as to what is fair and unfair in terms of international economic relationships, unequal market (equipment and services) entry opportunities have been created, and international telecommunications policy discussions have been expanded from technical debate towards economic and trade negotiations. Adequate multilateral structures in which to carry out this debate are lacking. Bilateralism has also tended to replace multilateral negotiations as reflected in United States-Japan discussions leading up to the restructuring of the telecommunications industry in Japan. There is an obvious need for further clarification and understanding of different policy positions. It is evident given in some cases the Consitutional responsibilities conferred on PTTs, that differences in structures may continue to occur but that judicious use of policies can curtail adverse spillover effects which may arise from different approaches.

International debate on telecommunications liberalisation is also clouded by the fear that because of differences in market size, deregulation could have a negative impact. The liberalisation issue is therefore sometimes viewed as more than competition versus monopoly, but the question of the impact of foreign service providers on the domestic service structure under conditions of liberal market entry. In the context of preparatory work for the World Administrative Telegraph and Telephone Conference (WATTC-88), under the auspices of the International Telecommunication Union, a concern has been expressed by several countries that private providers of new telecommunications services operating in a competitive environment may not be subject to obligations of telecommunications administrations which would sign the future convention which imposes international treaty obligations[27]. But the contrary position needs to be also posed. That is, by incorporating certain rights and obligations in treaty provisions, telecommunications administrations may be in a position to adversely affect the international growth and development of private service providers.

The decision of the ITU Plenipotentiary Conference in 1982 to work towards a "broad international regulatory framework for all existing and foreseen new telecommunications services"[28] was timely. There is a need for this framework to allow for the international development of information markets and the information industry which have the potential to emerge.

There are at present pressures being applied for movement toward competition in the provision of international switched and leased lines services where there is a need to achieve agreement among national governments and PTT administrations. In recent years, the United States has authorised new privately-owned high capacity fibre optic cables for trans-Atlantic services and five new separate satellite systems that would serve the United States-European market, although these services are still in the planning stage. New entrants intend to provide specialised services to high-volume users and are pressuring PTTs to reach satisfactory interconnection agreements.

Competition in the international area will be encouraged or discouraged by policies adopted in different countries. Competition could be limited to specialised services or extended to all services. The role of telecommunications as a stimulus to economic growth in OECD countries is particularly apparent in the Value-Added Network Services market. International resale of leased lines to customers other than those within the subscriber's customer base, currently restricted by the International Telecommunications Union CCITT regulations, can act as a bottleneck to the expansion of the international value-added services market by preventing connection of leased lines to public switched networks. Continuing controversy over market structure in new services areas, over competitive entry, and the boundaries of regulation, may provide a stimulus to development of intra-firm and closed user group networks, rendering many new service possibilities inaccessible to small and medium sized users.

For VANS there is a danger if no suitable multilateral framework emerges that bilateral negotiation of agreements between governments and PTTs may supercede multilateral decision-making. For example, Japan and the United States are discussing this possibility. Non-participating nations may be increasingly excluded from access to innovative service offerings. The implications for trade in information and transaction services and for businesses active in widely dispersed geographical markets could be far-reaching. International Value-Added Network Services that could be permitted on a selective bilateral basis could divert traffic in and out of OECD countries depending on domestic and international rates. Fluctuations in the flow of traffic of this kind could have second order effects on other domestic industries as markets tend to become more internationally linked.

5. Diversity of Solutions

There is a need to recognise the diversity which exists in economic structures, social and economic goals, and important size differences between national economies. Such differences may require the adoption of different options within the framework of telecommunications facility and service provision. As well, the rate of adjustment to new structures will invariably differ among countries. Genuine differences of opinion also exist as to the efficiency of the market, in certain circumstances, in providing the most desirable solution.

While recognizing the requirement for diversity, the increasing differences in regulatory regimes, which have widened in recent years by rapid changes in frameworks in the United States, United Kingdom and Japan, can have important international effects resulting in:

- Trade frictions, in equipment and services. This is particularly the case in value-added network services where different perceptions exist as to whether a service should be provided by private companies. In certain cases PTTs are entering into agreements with a range of service providers (e.g. electronic mail), but do not allow establishment of these companies in their domestic market;
- To the extent that the telecommunications sector is important in enhancing sectoral competitiveness, differences which may result from some countries adopting policies which allow for a relatively more dynamic and innovative telecommunications sector, could in the long-term also have trade spill-over effects as well as more general microeconomic and macroeconomic effects.

In certain cases international frictions may arise because of unilateral changes by one country which could be taken advantage of by foreign firms, whereas the countries of those firms do not provide reciprocity. This has been the case for equipment (Chapter IV) and is increasingly occurring in the service area. The inability to provide services on an international basis because of constraints by some countries may also impose economic costs. It needs to be recognised as well that the lack of regulations in countries may also constitute a trade impediment in the telecommunications service area (e.g. in value-added network services) : effective copyright legislation and data privacy protection regulations are two examples where service trade may be inhibited by differences in the regulatory regime.

Important international differences also arise because in countries where telecommunications was a regulated monopoly the response to changing technological and service possibilities came in the form of change to existing regulations. Whereas, where the monopoly was a state-owned public service the response was usually based on extending monopoly coverage. Questions of abuse of dominant position were not relevant to state monopolies since extension of the monopoly, it was argued, was a requirement in order to ensure that network integrity and universal service considerations were met.

Differences in perceptions of basic concepts also can create international misunderstandings. Thus, the United States' interpretation of deregulation implies, given the existence of private monopolies regulated by the state, easing of market entry and easing of other regulatory restrictions. In the European context and for some other Member countries deregulation does not have the implication of dismantling the monopoly, but rather restricting it or increasing its efficiency by subjecting it to the disciplines imposed by corporate responsibility. In Europe, pressure for change has not challenged the traditional monopoly structure of telecommunications basic services. Rather the emphasis has been on a redefinition of the boundary line between monopoly and competitive services. The question of foreign participation and/or ownership in network facilities will also have to be examined nationally and internationally given that important differences may arise.

6. Policy Formulation

The fundamental reason, historically, for regulation in telecommunications was the notion that a private industry serving the public, and therefore where public interest considerations arose, should be constrained by regulatory oversight in particular to prevent the abuse of dominant position and denial of access. The emerging concept of the industry as a natural monopoly gave a rationale for maintaining a monopoly market structure and reinforced the regulatory requirement in order to ensure that the monopoly was serving the public interest and supplying its service at least cost. The increasing availability of telephones and declining costs changed the perception of the telephone as a luxury to a necessity, and also provided a further rationale for regulation of the service industry in order to promote and protect universal service considerations with its concomitant aims regarding price, quality of service and protection of the network.

Differences in the type of ownership of the monopoly (private or public) were based on differences in national, legal, institutional and political traditions. Nationalisation by many countries in Europe of private telecommunications service providers in the late nineteenth and early twentieth century reflected the use of an instrument commonly thought of as optimal when public interest considerations were viewed as important. In turn, this implied that regulatory authority became the responsibility of the service provider itself or a co-partner, in terms of a government department. "Internalising" the regulatory function has been viewed as acceptable in that a public corporation in itself was mandated to serve the public interest and ministerial or legislative oversight considered sufficient.

A range of political economy theories have emerged to explain regulatory behaviour. Notions have emerged that regulation acts to transfer wealth, the outcome being domination by a small group implying that producers gain at the expense of consumers, the concept of regulation as a forum for arbitrating adversary claims has arisen, or that regulation provides stability and therefore helps reduce risk. Despite considerations as to the outcome of regulation the common thread within these theories is that regulation is aimed at altering the distributive outcome of market solutions.

It needs to be recognised that inherently there is a fundamental conflict between economic efficiency based on competition and regulation. Competition laws are often thought adequate to respond to market imperfections per se. In contrast, where public interest requirements need to be met such as in telecommunications, resort to regulation is needed. However, with regulation, not only is there the difficulty in balancing competing interests, but also in meeting conflicting objectives such as service efficiency and social goals.

Ineffective regulation creates difficulties which are amplified when there is rapid technological change as has occurred in the telecommunications service industry. This is because technological change can create new economic entry opportunities (e.g. microwave technology challenged existing long-distance technology in the late 1950s), can impose economic costs if the regulatory process is too slow to adjust to technological change and can change the structural supply characteristics of specific segments of the industry. The difficulties which technological change can lead to, are well illustrated in regulatory problems in the United States to come to grips with boundaries and definitions between basic and enhanced services (see Chapter II).

As the previous chapter showed, some OECD countries have already changed significantly their regulatory frameworks. Other countries have made more modest adjustments or are still actively considering change. As a result of diverging pressure group interests the issue of regulation, its framework and coverage in telecommunications has become politicised in many countries.

In most countries telephone administrations have, over the years, accumulated considerable powers, and in most cases PTTs have extended their monopolies beyond their original mandates. In many instances the telecommunications service monopolies have acted – in some cases de jure, in others de facto – as legislator, judge and regulator. A surprising concentration of power in countries which would not normally tolerate the merging of these three functions in other administrative entities. Political economy suggests that it is unlikely that a regulating authority will act against its own interests. There is therefore a strong case for separation of powers.

Irrespective of whether telecommunications services are considered as a natural monopoly or not, irrespective of equity considerations regarding universal telecommunications services, and irrespective of whether the latter function is bestowed on PTTs by legislation, constitutional power or administrative acts, there is no basis for allowing PTTs to set the rules, interpret these rules, and police them. Neutrality considerations argue strongly for an independent regulatory body to oversee the telecommunications administrations, ensure that they are fulfilling their mandatory requirements, ensuring that where competition exists that it is fair, and interpreting, telecommunications framework conditions. In short, the requirement for an arms length relationship between government and the telecommunications administration, as well as between the latter and independent regulatory bodies, is important.

Such independent regulatory bodies already exist in several countries : The Federal Communications Commission in the United States, the Canadian Radio-television and Telecommunications Commission, and the Office of the Director General of Telecommunications in the United Kingdom, set up by the Telecommunications Act of 1984 after privatisation of British Telecom. In France, as well, an independent agency, La Commission Nationale des Communications et des Libertés has been recently set up and is expected to expand its responsibility to cover telecommunications.

Although the importance of an independent regulatory authority needs to be stressed, it must also be recognised that major policy initiatives have not always – and cannot be expected to –come from such authorities. Government policy-makers must also play a major role, particularly as regards the broader framework conditions.

In this regard, there has been a notable lack of macroeconomic input in the policy process. Economics ministries have not recognised (or while recognising, have been unable to intervene effectively) the importance of telecommunications in economic structures in the 1990s, and their potential macroeconomic effects on productivity and growth in manufacturing and services. As shown earlier, telecommunications plays a fairly significant role in the economy.

There is, as well, an increasing need to address the trade spillover effects of telecommunications policy.

In the latter context there is a need to recognise that regulations may create barriers to trade. It is therefore important that regulations should not be overly excessive, that is, they should be "reasonable". The need for openness in the regulatory process, transparency of regulations and the opportunity for foreign and domestic interests to comment on regulations before their implementation is also important[29].

Economic regulation affects both market structures as well as conduct and performance of service providers in the market, in particular in that regulation impinges on the revenue of carriers. In this context the most commonly used methods have been regulation of the rate of return usually used in North America or regulation of prices. Extensive arguments can be made in support of either methodology. It needs to be recognised that "... the distinction between price-control regulation and rate of return regulation is not and cannot be clear-cut"[30]. As argued by the Office of Telecommunications in the United Kingdom, the use in that country of price-control regulation was favoured over rate-of-return regulation in that it was thought more efficient "in the circumstances that prevail in Britain at the present time"[31]. Member countries need to evaluate their own particular conditions and desired outcomes before opting for any particular system of regulation.

7. Future Telecommunications Structures

The existence of a range of new technologies is leading increasingly to facilities competition in telecommunications services. Such technologies as microwave transmission, satellites, fibre optics, cellular radio and copper-wire transmission have complementary features, but are also beginning to compete for traffic.

It is likely that at the international level the most intense facilities competition will occur over the transatlantic route which has the highest traffic density in the world. Facilities, planning and traffic distribution on this route have traditionally been managed by the North Atlantic Consultative Working Group (involving the FCC, Teleglobe and CEPT Administrations). Traffic was subject to balance loading, that is, split between cable and satellite systems.

As a result of liberalisation in the United States and the United Kingdom, several new optical fibre cable transmission lines are under construction or planned for the transatlantic route. The requirement on ATT with respect to allocation of traffic between satellites and cables is also changing[32], while in the United States liberalisation of satellite systems by private carriers could also add to new capacity on transatlantic routes.

There is little consensus as to the implications of the considerable expansion in capacity[33] on transatlantic routes. Some experts argue that demand will be stimulated by lower prices and new service availabilities and potential. There appears to be a longer-run trend for satellite transmission to cater for broadcasting markets and serving less dense communications routes, while fibre cable will be used for dense traffic routes and for point-to-point transmission.

An important aspect of the growth of new services and facilities is also the longer-term potential competition between cellular telephony systems and basic telephone services as well as the potential for cellular technology to complement existing technology used for basic telecommunications services.

Policy issues that arise with respect to the future structure of the telecommunications services industry are concerned centrally with the characteristics of network facilities, their accessibility and use. A wide variety of technical and administrative options remain open to PTTs as they plan for the medium and long-term modernisation of existing telecommunications infrastructures. The balance that will be achieved among services provided over public switched and leased line networks will be dependent on the nature of demand for new, and in some cases, unforeseen services. The resolution of policy questions concerning the introduction of the ISDN and relative prices charged for switched and leased line services, carry implications for PTT future investment programmes.

Most PTTs see the ISDN in the 1990s as enabling them to offer diverse packages of services ranging from basic voice telephone to specialised value-added services, eventually reducing the demand for leased line capacity. Some experts foresee a further evolution of telecommunication networks providing switched wideband capability on an end-to-end basis[34].

Forecasts of this kind imply a future industry structure in which network facilities are offered by PTTs on a monopoly basis. The distribution of responsibility for service provision would then become a policy issue to determine access to network capacity. The outcome will be dependent, to a large extent, on the responsiveness of PTTs to demand from large business users and the extent to which these users chose alternative methods of supply.

In the telecommunications policy area several issues need to be addressed. For example, is there sufficient evidence of demand for narrow or wideband switched capacity throughout the telecommunications system? What are the relative costs of providing services over switched versus leased-line networks. It may be that as an alternative to extensive network redesign and upgrading, specialised leased line and closed user networks could be developed that provide high quality services at lower cost. A small proportion of large users may find it more efficient to by-pass the public switched network.

The alternative structures for the telecommunication services industry will be largely dependent on the answers to these questions and the form that policy responses take in each OECD country. The balance that is achieved between divergent development trends carries implications for PTT investment plans, prices of telecommunications services, and national and international agreements as to access to network facilities.

NOTES AND REFERENCES

1. See Marcellus S. Snow, ed., Telecommunications Regulation and Deregulation in Industrialized Democracies, Longman, New York, 1985; and Encaoua, D., Réglementation and Concurrence : Quelques Eléments de Théorie Economique, Document de Travail, Direction de la Prévision, Ministère de l'Economie, des Finances et de la Privatisation, France, 1986.

2. A market is considered as having natural monopoly characteristics if the relative cost function is subadditive up to the relevant output level; that is, if the costs of production of a single firm for a range of products or services is less than the cost of production of the same range of products or services by many different independent firms. The above assumptions pertain to a static framework.

3. In a situation with a single output natural monopoly characteristics are equivalent to economies of scale; that is, average costs decline as the level of output increases.

4. See, for example, L. Courville (ed.), Economic Analysis of Telecommunications, North Holland, 1983. F. Kiss and B. Lefebvre, Econometric models of telecommunications firms, A Survey, Revue Economique No.2, Mars 1987.

5. Baumol, W.J., Panzar, J.C., Willig, R.D., Contestable Markets and the Theory of Industrial Structure; Harcourt, Bruce, Janovich, 1982.

6. See, for example, Shepherd, W.G., "Contestability" vs. Competition, American Economic Review, Vol. 74, No. 4, September 1984; Vickers, J. and Yarrow, G., Privatisation and the Natural Monopolies, Public Policy Centre, London 1985; Trebing, H.M., Apologetics of Deregulation in Energy and Telecommunications : An Institutionalist Assessment, Journal of Economic Issues, Vol. XX, No. 3, September 1986.

7. Snow, M.S., Regulation to Deregulation : the Telecommunications Sector and Industrialization, Telecommunications Policy, December 1985.

8. Neuman, Karl-Heinz and Wieland, Bernhard. "Competition and Social Objectives : The Case of West German Telecommunications", Diskussionsbeitrage zur Telecommunikationsforschung, Nr. 14, September 1985, p. 7.

9. Bell Canada; evidence submitted to CRTC "Interchange Competition and Related Issues", CRTC Telecommunications Public Notice 1984-86, 30th April 1984, p. 5, cited in R. Mansell "Telecommunications Bypass Threat : Real or Imagined", Journal of Economics Issues, Vol. 22(1), March 1986, p. 157.

10. In Europe telex traffic diversion has occurred but it would be difficult to detect voice and data traffic diversion.

11. It could be argued that despite competition there has been increased regulation.

12. This in turn led to protests both as a result of the increase in monthly charges, but also because the flat rate discriminated against infrequent long-distance users and in favour of intense users who, as concerns residential customers are normally in the medium-to-higher income brackets.

13. By-pass is defined by the Federal Communications Commission as communications traffic that originates or terminates either without using the facilities of the local exchange carrier, or by using carrier-provided leased lines.

14. This suggestion was not an official proposal, but put forward in an academic paper. The underlying theory of such arguments is that competition is the most efficient discovery procedure to unveil cost and competitive conditions.

15. It is revealing that nearly every PTT annual report tries to compare local charges to increases in the Consumer Price Index. At times however, charges were effectively increased by reducing the time duration for each measured call – an increase not accounted for in making comparisons with the CPI. Estimates for Canada indicate that the index for average weekly wages increased from 100 in 1951 to 668 in 1983, whereas the indexes for monthly telephone rental for residential and business customers rose to 252 and 330 respectively over the same period. (R. Pike and V. Mosco, Canadian Consumers and Telephone Pricing : from luxury to necessity and back again; Telecommunications Policy, March 1986.)

16. Effective as from 1st January 1986.

17. This process started in 1959 as a result of 27 FCC 405 (1959), Allocation of Microwave Frequencies in the Band Above 890 Mhz.

18. See Telecommunications Reports, Vol. 52(29), 21st July 1986, pp. 14-17.

19. Denious, R.D., "The Subsidy Myth : Who Pays for the Local Loop?", Telecommunications Policy, September 1986.

20. Melody, W.H., "Cost Standards for Judging Local Exchange Rates", in Diversification, Deregulation and Increased Uncertainty in Public Utility Industries, Proceedings of the Institute of Public Utilities, Thirteenth Annual Conference, MSU Public Utilities Papers, 1983.

21. R. Mansell, op-cit.

22. Nynex (U.S.), for example, had in 1985 a 6 per cent increase in local service revenues – of this 58 per cent came from rate increases, 29 per cent from increased demand, and 13 per cent from restructuring toll calls as local calls (Nynex Annual Report, 1985).

23. From 91.9 per cent to 92.2 per cent.

24. No thorough analysis has been made by opponents of deregulation in the United States to indicate the thresholds at which customers would start to drop-off the system at a significant rate. A recent study by the Florida Public Service Commission found that significant increases in telephone service rates would lead to only a slight drop-off in subscribers. The study found that this applies as well to low-income subscribers for whom connection charges and deposits were a greater barrier (cited in Communications Week, 23rd June 1986).

25. Reference can be made to the Televerket (Swedish Telecommunications Administration), which has historically been operated as a public service corporation rather than as a State authority. Sweden, it should be recalled, has the highest penetration rates for main lines in the OECD.

26. Public Policy Center, Privatisation and the National Monopolies, London, 1985.

27. Rutkowski, A.M., Regulations for Integrated Services Networks : WATTC-88, INTERMEDIA, May 1986, Volume 14, No. 3.

28. World Administrative Telegraph and Telephone Conference, Final Acts of the Plenipotentiary Conference, Nairobi, 1982.

29. See OECD, Elements of a conceptual framework for trade in services, 1987.

30. Office of Telecommunications, United Kingdom, November 1986, Review of British Telecom's Tariff Charges, a report issued by the Director General of Telecommunications.

31. Ibid.

32. AT&T had traditionally been required to allocate 52 per cent of traffic to satellite and 48 per cent to cables. Proposals freeing AT&T from loading cable or satellite circuits are as yet not complete. The FCC has issued a notice of proposed rulemaking for developing post - 1988 loading policy.

33. Planned fibre optic capacity for the North Atlantic includes (completion dates in brackets) *Source*: FINTECH : 59/9.:

TAT-8   (1988) :   7 500 64 kbit/sec paths
PTAT-1 (1989) : 12 000 64 kbit/sec paths
TAT-9   (1991) : 15 000 64 kbit/sec paths
PTAT-2 (1992) : 12 000 64 kbit/sec paths

34. Solomon, R.J., "Changing the Nature of Telecommunications Networks", *Intermedia*, Vol. 14(3), May 1986, pp. 30-33.

Chapter IV

STRUCTURAL CHARACTERISTICS AND CHANGE IN THE TELECOMMUNICATIONS EQUIPMENT INDUSTRY

1. Introduction

The value of the world telecommunications equipment market[1] is variously estimated as ranging between $70 billion and $80 billion[2]. Roughly, the OECD area accounts for approximately 90 per cent of this market with the United States 40 per cent, Japan around 12 per cent and Europe 25 per cent – within Europe no individual country has a market larger than 5-6 per cent of the world total.

Estimates of the long-term growth of the equipment market vary (the U.S. Department of Commerce estimates 9 per cent for the U.S. market over 1986-1990 and Arthur D. Little Inc. 8.3 per cent for world markets), but remain consistent in that all predictions are for high rates of growth often at levels twice that of projections for growth in the volume of GDP.

In view of the range of equipment in the telecommunications industry, each with its own market and growth characteristics, it is not possible to cover all aspects and issues related to the equipment industry. Rather the broad structural characteristics and changes which influence the industry will be examined. It is useful, however, to distinguish between terminal equipment markets which are increasingly being opened to competition in many countries and where demand is much more diffuse, and network markets for switching equipment and transmission.

2. The Industry Structure

The major market for the network equipment industry has been the monopoly suppliers of telecommunications services. This monopsonist structure, and the fact that demand for equipment is derived, based on the rate of network expansion, has resulted at the *national* level in a high degree of concentration in equipment firms' market share with regard to common carrier equipment (Table IV-1). In some cases equipment suppliers were in a monopoly position and in most cases operated in a duopoly market structure. Monopoly telecommunications service providers have, and are, also involved in equipment supply. The structure of telecommunications equipment markets is closely linked to that of the service industry and the regulatory framework. As such, regulatory changes impacting on the service structure have important impacts on the equipment market structure.

Irrespective of whether a service monopoly is justified or not the procurement of equipment from monopoly/duopoly suppliers or on the basis of self-supply is not economically justified by service requirements. The rationale for procurement practices are weak commonly including:

Table IV-1. **Central switching markets:
approximate firm market share in 1985**

Country	Firm	Percentage share
Austria	Siemens EWSD ITT (under licence to Siemens) }	50
	Local manufacturers (under licence to Northern Telecom)	50
Belgium	ITT (S12)	80
	GTE	20
Denmark	Ericsson (AXE)	80
	ITT (S12)	20
Finland	Telenokia (GTE licencee)	50
	Ericsson	35
	Siemens	15
France	CIT-Alcatel (E 10/MT25) Thomson (MT) }	84
	CGCT (MT25) }	16
Germany	Siemens (EWSD)	60
	ITT (S 12)	40
Ireland	CIT-Alcatel (E10)	40
	Ericsson (AXE)	40
Italy	Italtel (+ GTE)	60
	Others (ITT, Ericsson)	40
Netherlands	Phillips-ATT	75
	Ericsson (AXE) ITT }	25
Norway	ITT (S 12)	100
Spain	ITT (S 12)	70
	Ericsson (AXE)	30
Sweden	Ericsson (AXE)	25
	Teli (AXE)	75
United Kingdom	GEC	29
	Plessey	44

Source: OECD, Claude Labarrère, L'Europe des Postes et des Télécommunications, Masson, 1985, and other sources.

- The need to ensure that equipment specifications are available and meet service requirements and standards;
- Stability of supply;
- National interest.

In reality telecommunications administrations in most major equipment producing countries took on an industrial policy role in developing, protecting and administering an equipment industry. The need for a minimum of price and product competition was recognized by splitting procurement between two or several firms, ignoring, however, that procurement on such a basis seldom achieves the desired competitive effects which would arise from an open market. The requirement to reduce total life-time costs of equipment requires that long-term

71

software and hardware support and training be made available for switching equipment, limiting flexibility in changing suppliers in the shorter term. However, contracts awarded through competitive procurement procedures can also ensure that these long-run maintenance costs of successful bidders are minimized.

The logic of universal service requirements and network efficiency should lead to policies aimed at long-term cost minimisation in equipment purchases and in maximising consumer equipment choice. Few telephone administrations can insist that their mandates require them to take an active role in support of the equipment industry.

As a result of procurement policies the competitive domain for the industry has been limited to non-producing OECD countries and Third World markets[3]. In many OECD countries, which are not producing equipment or all ranges of equipment, close ties are often maintained with one or several producing companies often on the basis of some offset arrangements. In many markets open to competition outside the OECD, the governments have often assisted their domestic companies in promoting sales of equipment, especially on the basis of favourable export financing arrangements[4]. Procurement practices have in some cases been detrimental to the competitive position of firms by orienting producers towards domestic markets and away from export markets, and by concentrating their equipment development and product specifications to meet PTT requirements which can differ from international requirements.

Although procurement by telecommunication administrations remains a driving force in equipment markets, its relative role is declining. This decline results in some cases from liberalisation in network attachment regulations especially for customer premises equipment, as well as the emergence of new equipment, or equipment for new service areas over which – in some cases – PTTs have not extended their monopolies.

For firms producing central office switches, the key product area of the equipment industry, there are several forces at play which can be expected to alter the structure of production[5]. Firstly, the current total production capacity of central office digital switches exceeds total world demand. There are fifteen manufacturers of large telephone exchanges in the OECD area from eight Member countries[6]. The success of these companies is varied both in terms of capacity installed as well as in the number of markets they have entered (Table IV-2).

Cost and competitive factors have already led to structural changes in the market and to strategic decisions by firms. These include the abandonment of Switzerland's IFS digital switching system, in which approximately SFr.300 million was invested over 1969-1983; the APT joint venture (AT&T and Philips) and abandonment by Philips of its own system, the takeover of Stromberg-Carlson by Plessey, and the Siemens-GTE co-operative agreement whereby Siemens has taken control of the non-United States operations of GTE's public switching and communications branches (GTE operations in Belgium, Italy and Taiwan will be subject to a separate agreement). The unsuccessful attempted takeover of Plessey by GEC (UK) was also partly based on telecommunications equipment supply considerations. The Monopolies and Mergers Commission of the United Kingdom turned down the take-over bid as being against the public interest, but recognized that there could be a need for the public switching activities of the two companies to be merged. The shift of assets between Thomson and CGE in France, Alcatel the new ITT-CGE joint venture, and the purchase of CGCT shares by Matra-Ericsson in France, and the merger between Italtel and Telettra in Italy, are also indicative of such structural change.

These decisions have been driven by the high development costs for digital switches (ranging from $500 million to $1 billion), a large percentage of which is accounted for by software costs – 75 to 80 per cent according to some estimates[7]. There is also an important

Table IV-2. **Market penetration by digital switch producers**
(As of end 1984)

Company	Product	Operating since	Number of lines installed	Number of national markets
Alcatel-Thomson	E10,MT 20/25	1979	8.7 million	45
Northern Telecom	DMS 100	1979	6.6	11
Ericsson	AXE	1977	4.2	59
AT&T	4ESS,5ESS	1976	4.0	8
NEC	NEAX 61	1979	1.7	37
GTE	GTD-3EAX-&-5EAX	1978	1.3	5
ITT	SYSTEM 12	1978	0.93	
Stromberg-Carlson	System Century	1977	0.9	
Siemens	EWSD	1980	0.12	15

Source: VECKANS Affärer, 18th April 1985.

cost requirement in changing switches to meet requirements of different markets[8]. Greater international co-operation in the future on standards and in the framework of the Open Systems Interconnection may help partially reduce such high costs of market entry.

Although it is expected that significant adjustments will have to take place in the structure of the telecommunications equipment industry, such changes are likely to be phased rather than dramatic mainly as a result of expectations that markets will only be liberalised slowly in Europe. It is estimated that about 8 per cent of the *world* digital market is required for a firm to stay viable – a handful of existing firms have attained such a share. The requirement for firms over the next several years to develop a new generation of digital switches for ISDN (and for Integrated Broadband Communications Networks), and related costs for such systems, will require firms to obtain a significantly higher world market share to remain viable – some estimates indicate a minimum of 16 per cent.

Rationalisation is required foremost in the number of competing switching *systems*, especially in Europe where seven systems are competing for a quarter of the world market. Such rationalisation is likely to occur through shared development costs and the move towards compatible standards. Ultimately, however, production rationalisation may be required and will be more difficult to achieve given the instinct of most countries in Europe to protect their manufacturing base. In many cases firms are aware of this need for rationalisation and are actively trying to pursue such a policy, whereas government policies often act to deter such moves.

A second, and related, factor altering the equipment industry's structure is the liberalisation of markets, especially in the United States, United Kingdom and Japan. In the United States the break-up of AT&T as a result of deregulation has already led to a reduction of the dominant share of Western Electric (since 1984 AT&T Network Systems) of the United States market. For example, in 1985, of the 17 million *digital* lines installed by United States common carriers market shares were:

AT&T	24.3%
Northern Telecom	43.7
GTE	17.1
Plessey/Stromberg	6.1
ITT (U.S.)	5.8
NEC	3.0

Source: Communications Week of 17th March 1986.

The telecommunications industry in the United States has traditionally been highly concentrated, with the two largest service operating companies (AT&T and GTE) owning the two largest manufacturing companies. The concentration ratio for the four largest firms is estimated at 85 per cent[9]. There has been a significant growth in the number of establishments producing telecommunications equipment in the United States – from 90 in 1963 to 270 in 1981[10] – spurred on by product innovation and by the liberalisation of the terminal equipment market[11].

The value of telecommunications equipment shipments of the United States grew at an annual average rate of 11.5 per cent over the 1973-86 period (Table 12). Exports, which represented 2.2 per cent of shipment in 1973, have remained relatively unimportant in growth, accounting for 4.1 per cent of shipments by 1986. Imports, on the other hand, which represented only 3.8 per cent of apparent consumption of equipment in 1981 have accelerated since then, accounting for 10 per cent of consumption by 1986.

Much of the import penetration cannot be directly attributed to the divestiture of 1984. However, the United States, given the size of its telecommunications market and ease of entry, is obviously the most attractive market for foreign firms. The 1984 divestiture had the important result of opening up the central office switch market and transmission equipment markets to increased competition, and accelerating investment in these areas, as the seven BOCs tried to build up their networks. The already keen competition for central office switch markets can be expected to become more fierce, as a result of the expected decline in demand for net additions of lines from present levels (15 to 17 million per year) to about 6 million by 1989. Such a decline in the level of demand may also lead to major consequences for firms concentrating on the production of central office switches. For example, current annual production capacity of AT&T and Northern Telecom in the United States is 8 million and 6 million lines respectively.

Divestiture also had the important consequence of freeing AT&T from constraints prohibiting it from acting as a competitive seller of equipment on international markets. Active pursuit of new markets by AT&T (through its joint venture with Philips) has already led to some success in obtaining markets in other OECD countries. As this company adjusts its internal structure to reflect marketing requirements[12] – after being a monopoly equipment provider with a stable market – it is likely to create additional adjustment pressures in the international central office switch market[13].

Divestiture, while leading to domestic changes, is also likely to create international pressures for change in other national equipment markets. It will become, for example, increasingly difficult for firms from countries with markets closed to competition, to establish a long-term position in the United States market if their national markets do not provide a reciprocal opportunity to United States firms[14]. In recognition of this, some firms (e.g. Siemens) are planning to set up production in the United States.

An important aspect of competitive markets such as in the United States, is that they are driven by user requirements rather than pushed along by planned network developments of the monopoly service providers. In terms of equipment demand and product innovation this has important dynamic consequences. Witness the rapid changes in the composition of equipment demand in the United States:

Japan, OECD's second largest national market for equipment, has been effectively closed to foreign competition until April 1985. The United States-Japan Procurement Agreement signed in 1981 with respect to NTT had, in reality, led to only a minor share by United States firms in NTT procurement. Traditionally Nippon Telegraph and Telephone purchased from a large number of Japanese companies although the top ten suppliers accounted for just under two-thirds of NTT procurement and the top four suppliers around

Market breakdown, actual and estimated

(In percent)

	1983	1985 est.	1987 est.
Terminal equipment	12.5	15.3	14.6
Data communications equipment	9.0	13.6	15.1
Switching systems	40.0	29.9	25.5
Transmission equipment	17.5	15.6	15.2
Carrier switching equipment	15.5	14.0	11.1
Other (including cellular mobile radio)	5.5	11.6	18.5
$ million	14 807	21 238	27 333

Source: Dataquest.

45 per cent (i.e. Nippon Electric Company, Fujitsu, Oki Electronics and Hitachi).

The value, in yen, of production of telecommunications equipment in Japan increased at an annual average growth rate of 8.7 per cent over 1973-84. The period was characterized by a high growth rate in exports of equipment at a rate of 26.5 per cent resulting in exports increasing from 6.7 per cent of production in 1973 to 23 per cent by 1984 (Table 13). In stark contrast to this export ratio, the ratio of imports in apparent consumption of equipment has remained insignificant – 1.1 per cent in 1984 (admittedly a threefold increase in percentage points from 1973).

Underlying this export-led growth in production was a fundamental change in the product composition of output (Table 13) away from carrier transmission and switching equipment to equipment demanded by the private sector. It is in the latter sector, customer premises equipment, where export markets have been most open to penetration, especially in the United States. In 1982, for the first time in Japan itself, private sector demand for telecommunications equipment was larger than NTT demand. This resulted from increasing trends in office automation and also because investment by the NTT, which had previously been growing *steadily*, declined abruptly by 16 per cent over 1981/82.

In terms of import penetration all evidence points to the fact that United States' firms encountered difficulty in penetrating the Japanese market for line equipment. In some cases, however, lack of import penetration must be placed in context with the emphasis placed on satisfying domestic demand by United States firms, especially in recent years, and their export performance in general. It is clear that United States' firms were not well placed to deliver products in demand which resulted in the import surge in 1983-84 in the United States.

The largest contract awarded to a foreign company by NTT[15] was at the end of 1985 to Northern Telecom. This contract – worth $250 million over 7 years for the DMS-10 digital switch – is, however, expected to form only a small percentage of NTT equipment purchases over the period. The performance of NTT in purchasing foreign central office switches is not different from that of PTTs in major European economies, and only since divestiture has there been any important penetration in the United States by foreign central office switch producers[16].

Although the EEC (10) has a potential market equal to one quarter of the total OECD market, in fact this market is ten distinct markets, dominated by the four largest markets of Germany, France, the United Kingdom and Italy. Little import penetration of firms from the major producing countries in markets of other equipment producing countries has occurred.

Despite recognition by Member states of the fragmentation of the EEC market and the need to create a pan-European equipment market, this concept is far from becoming a reality. Despite various initiatives, declarations[17] and avowals in support of the principle of open intra-EEC markets, increasing divergencies in the market structure of Member states and in firm strategies, is making it increasingly difficult to fulfil such proposals. Concrete actions have had a longer-term perspective such as through R & D programmes (ESPRIT, RACE) and agreements towards harmonized standards.

This inability in the EEC to open PTT procurement to firms of the Member states has already led to doubts as to whether an EEC-based equipment industry can, in the long-term, become a competitive force in world markets. The APT joint venture and market penetration in the Netherlands, the British Telecom purchase of Ericsson and APT switches and purchases by Mercury Communications of Northern Telecom Switches bear witness to the failure by European firms (and policy-makers) to co-operate in marketing and product development.

The importance of rapidly obtaining an open European market for central switching equipment needs stressing if a competitive world-scale equipment industry is to remain viable in the longer-term. The most compelling arguments for this are the significant economies of scale in R & D[18] and in production. Oftel has estimated that the:

".... incremental cost per line over 1 million lines is only a little over half average cost per line for the first 1 million"[19].

Policy-makers in the individual EEC states are increasingly finding themselves stuck more firmly on the horns of a dilemma. They are concerned that opening their procurement market to competition many irreversibly weaken their domestic producing company or at least dilute its national identity. But delaying domestic competition and relying on export markets alone to provide the production scale needed to remain competitive is increasingly likely to lead to retaliatory action[20]. The lack of faith in the ability of their domestic firms to survive the forces of open market competition is increasingly becoming a reality as a result of deliberate protectionist policies. With investment geared toward digitalisation important market opportunities still exist for manufacturers in different countries of Europe (Table IV.3). The extent to which these markets become open to competition may play an important role in the future structure of the industry.

Table IV-3. **Distribution of central switching eauipment by type: 1985**

Percentage distribution

	Step-by-step	Crossbar	Other electro-mechanical	Space-division switching	Digital electronic
Belgium	–	–	58.23	39.14	2.63
France	0.01	50.24	–	14.95	34.80
Italy	61.43	30.69	3.23	1.72	2.93
Norway	12.19	71.62	–	11.0	–
Netherlands	39.60	10.41	5.89	–	5.05
Portugal	–	57.47	42.47	–	–
Spain	13.71	76.36	–	–	1.79
United Kingdom	–	17.39	49.30	0.34	0.05
Sweden	56.86	–	25.18	–	17.97
Switzerland	77.37	22.63	–	–	–
Germany	98.82	–	–	1.18	–

Source: STET

In *France* the decision to rapidly build up the telecommunications infrastructure taken in the early 1970s was linked to an industrial policy initiative to develop the equipment industry. French PTT purchases are made through government sanctioned cartels which have jurisdiction over co-ordinated R&D, technical specifications and distribution of government investment funds. This policy was successful in buiding up the equipment industry – telecommunications equipment sales in France have increased rapidly at an annual average rate of 15.6 per cent over 1972-84 (Table 14) with exports playing a key role growing at 22.1 per cent over the period and accounting for 18 per cent of sales by 1984. Imports, however, remain low and account for less than 5 per cent of apparent domestic consumption of equipment.

Since 1981 sales growth has accelerated mainly as a result of private sector demand. The public sector has since then also shown a relative decline in importance as network investment has slowed down. This slowdown, shown below in terms of DGT purchases of main lines, has reduced the share of the PTT in total sales by domestic producers from 71 per cent in 1972 to 52 per cent in 1982 and 48 per cent by 1985:

Purchase of main lines by the DGT
('000)

1981	1982	1983	1984	1985	1986
1 845	1 735	1 465	1 143	1 014	900

Reduced levels of demand from the public sector implies a much greater reliance on export markets or to domestic private service sector expansion for continued growth by the equipment industry. As regards the latter market this implies the need for greater liberalisation of this market.

One result of French policy has been to reduce and eliminate foreign market share in the central switch market:

Market Share	1960	1976	1985
French firms	34%	83%	100%
Foreign firms	66%	17%	–

Source: Aurelle, Bruno, "Les Télécommunications", Editions La Découverte, Paris 1986.

This reduction was achieved largely as a result of the purchase by Thomson of the French subsidiaries of LMT (ITT International) and SFT (Ericsson) in 1976, followed in 1982 by the purchase by the state of CGCT from ITT[21]. The French telecommunications industry has, however, been heavily subsidised by the state – it is estimated that over 1982-87 some FF 55 billion will have been transferred from the "filière électronique" to support the industry. Contracts such as that by the PTT to Alcatel to provide terminals for the electronic telephone directory have provided a large home market and allowed Alcatel to lower production costs and enter export markets. Reportedly the contract accounts for one-quarter of Alcatel's turnover.

The *German* equipment industry structure is fairly similar to France. Equipment production has grown at 7.5 per cent over 1970-83 (Table 15) with growth in domestic

77

demand and exports at approximately the same level as production over the period. Exports constitute about one quarter of domestic production and have retained a fairly constant share in production. Similarly imports constitute a small percentage of domestic equipment consumption – a share which has remained constant over the period. The share of telephone equipment has remained steady in total equipment production, however telegraph equipment's share has declined steadily while that of transmissin equipment has increased to nearly 20 per cent of production. The German market is dominated by two major firms (Siemens and ITT's subsidiary SEL) and some other small producers. The major four domestic equipment suppliers have traditionally accounted for 90 per cent of total domestic equipment sales.

The *United Kingdom* telecommunications equipment market, as in many other European equipment producing countries, has traditionally been divided between two firms – Plessey and GEC – in order to ensure some price and quality competition. Sales of telegraph and telephone equipment have risen rapidly as a result of domestic demand (Table 16). Unlike other European countries export performance has been poor. A decision to develop a new digital exchange system (System X) was taken in the early 1970s but the position of the U.K. industry in the world digital exchange market has weakened as a result of development and delivery delays. No overseas exports of note have been made and delays have also led British Telecom, since privatisation, to order from non-U.K. suppliers. In *Sweden* the telecommunications administration, Televerket, produces about three-quarters of its equipment requirements in its own manufacturing branch, Teli. Ericsson, which does not directly rely on the Swedish telecommunications administration for sales, is an example of a firm which has been successful internationally despite – or because of – a small home market. Production growth has been buoyed by export markets and, although the export ratio has increased, there has been a rapid increase in the proportion of imports in consumption. Shipments of communications equipment expanded rapidly in *Canada* (15.5 per cent annual average growth between 1977-82) pulled along mainly by export growth (29 per cent over the 1977-82 period) based in particular on the success of Northern Telecom and Mitel in the United States market. Unlike most OECD countries Canada's market is characterized by high import penetration ratios and high export ratios, 66.5 and 56.0 respectively in 1983. The distortion of telecommunications policy for industrial policy purposes, which occurs in many OECD countries, is well illustrated in *Australia* where Telecom Australia is the largest user of electronic products and accounts for over 75 per cent of the market for telecommunications equipment and purchases 90 per cent of local output of telephone and telegraph equipment. High tariff protection is given to this market (being reduced to 20 percent) and the policy of Telecom is to arrange for the maximum practical Australian manufacturing content – obviously not a policy consistent with public service considerations to provide a universal service at a reasonable price. Despite tariffs, import penetration in Australia is relatively high by OECD standards. It should be noted that tariff protection is often more transparent than non-tariff barriers which are used in many other OECD countries. Offset policies are used for large government contracts awarded to external suppliers.

*

* *

The previous discussion has focussed on the central switch market but as already indicated this is not the fastest growing market, although it will remain important in terms of volume. The customer premises equipment market will be the main area affected by telecommunications liberalisation in the short term, particularly in Europe where it has lagged relative to the United States. One estimate for product growth rates is provided as follows:

Outlook for equipment markets

Percentage Annual Average Growth : 1983-90

	Total equipment	Public switching	Transmission	Private switching	Telex	Data transmission
Europe	6.8	4.3	9.1	10.9	10.7	13.9
North America	8.9	8.4	13.3	7.4	7.8	16.6
Oceania	7.4	5.4	10.2	10.8	7.4	6.3
Asia	7.4	4.3	10.1	10.2	7.7	20.7
World	7.9	6.1	10.9	9.6	9.0	15.7

Source: Italtel.

Some highlights:

– The private branch exchange market has shown important growth in major OECD countries but this growth is slowing down, particularly in the United States. Although in the United States historically AT&T had about 85 per cent of the market share, complete liberalisation of the market regarding attachment requirements in the mid-1970s coupled with the emergence of digital PBXs led to rapid growth of the market and competitors to AT&T[22]. Northern Telecom now has an equivalent market share to AT&T (about one-fifth each) closely followed by Rolm. Important market segmentation exists between large and smaller systems. Country market size differences are also important:

PABX Markets : 1984

('000 lines shipped)

U.S	U.K.	Germany	France	Italy
4 640	1 300	1 300	930	550

Sources: Northern Business Information; Les Echos of 5th December 1985.

– In countries where the telephone set market has been liberalised there has been important growth in equipment sales illustrated below for the United States. In Japan liberalisation of telephone sets in 1985 is estimated to generate total demand of about Y120 billion over 3 years. However, after consumers purchase leased telephones the market is likely to reach a saturation level:

Telephone sales in the United States

	1982	1983	1984	1985	1986 est.
$ million	400	925	1250	970	966
Number of sets	5 700	19 700	30 300	26 000	26 500

Source: Department of Commerce.

- The market for optical fibre cables has experienced significant growth over the last several years, driven by requirements for public networks (new demand and replacement for existing copper-wire transmission systems), office and manufacturing local area networks and military requirements. Existing investment initiatives indicate that this market will remain buoyant into the early 1990s.
- The market for mobile cellular telephony equipment is growing rapidly and growth is expected to continue, particularly once sufficient production volume is attained to enable prices to drop. Although in most countries the market is expected to come under some form of regulation, such regulation is not expected to be restrictive. The need to resolve questions of conflicting standards is more likely to slow market growth, especially in the European Community.

3. Employment

In most telecommunications equipment producing countries there has been an increase in employment in the industry during the 1970s, and since the end of that decade a decline in the labour force, in some cases a significant decline. Two factors account for these changes. Firstly, the acceleration and then slowdown in the build-up of the network had a direct impact on equipment production and employment. Secondly, as equipment became increasingly electronic and digital the labour-intensity of production declined, especially since assembly was susceptible to semi-automatic production techniques. Assembly times have been reduced from around 10 hours per main line to 20 minutes. Changing employment requirements are illustrated for a minimum size plant (500 000 lines of switches per year):

Employment

Manufacturing function	Crossbar	Stored programme control – analogue	Digital
Material (components, bond metal fabrications)	1 000	150	20
Assemble, wire	2 000	900	50
Test	250	200	50
Total:	3 250	1 250	120

Source: Cable and Wireless Ltd.

Table 17 illustrates employment trends in several countries. Expectations are for continued decline in employment over 1986/87, particularly as a result of changes in the labour-intensity of production, as well as in the longer-term, as structural adjustment takes place in the switching market.

Underlying aggregate employment data show that an important change has taken place in the composition of the labour force. For example, in France the blue collar work force in the equipment industry increased over the 1972-1977 period from 34 000 to 40 200, declining by the end of 1984 to 21 000. The net decline in white collar workers during the same period was 2 500. These trends reflect the increasing "knowledge-intensity" of the industry, particularly as regards software requirements. Ericsson in Sweden estimate that the labour content of telecommunications products will be reduced by 25 per cent over the next 2 to 3 years. The manpower implication of the R & D intensity of equipment will have perhaps more longer-term significance than any other production factor in altering the structure of the industry.

Data on labour productivity for the industry as measured by output per man (see below) show considerable variation. The data reflect differences in the output composition of the industry as well as differences in scale economies.

Output per man in U.S. dollars

(Deflated using GDP price index : in exchange rates and prices of 1980)

	France	Canada	United States
1973	37 775		61 015
1974	39 649		63 494
1976	41 846		75 659
1978	46 584	42 537	80 429
1980	49 780	45 965	80 439
1982	58 246	46 945	84 053
1983	63 749	43 814	86 836
1984	68 881	46 340	90 904

4. Trade in Telecommunications Equipment

One of the main international issues which has arisen from changes in telecommunications market structures has been in the area of trade in equipment. The ability to set-up new services is often based on the ability to obtain and interconnect appropriate equipment and equipment imports are often dependent on domestic service market regulations. Unilateral changes in service market structures which have led to the opening of such markets to competition have also stimulated trade in equipment and have led to bilateral pressures to open telecommunications markets for telecommunications equipment and services.

It is widely recognised that domestic telecommunications policies play a primary role in influencing the pattern and growth in demand for equipment and, as a result, equipment trade. Further, the emphasis given by some countries in promoting their domestic telecommunications equipment industry – directly and indirectly – has obvious implications for trade in equipment. The fact that international commercial relations in the telecommunications equipment industry reflect a wide range of domestic policy measures including regulatory and institutional frameworks governing telecommunications services, industrial policy initiatives, and direct or indirect trade measures provides a further complicating factor in international trade relations.

Recent experience has shown that trends towards the deregulation of the telecommunications service structure can have a significant impact on equipment markets and equipment trade. For example, in the United States the Federal Communications Commission First Order (1974) and Second Order (1977) registration programme led to significant growth in the interconnect market for customer premises equipment: it is estimated that sales grew from $300 million in 1975 to $1.4 billion by 1981[23]. Similarly, when the new Japanese Telecommunications Business Law (1985) came into effect, a large number of firms indicated their intention of setting up value added network services which are expected to have an important stimulus on equipment sales. This is also the case in the United Kingdom.

Regulatory changes can also lead to a redirection of marketing effort by equipment suppliers who have been tied closely to service providers. Obvious examples include the United Kingdom, the United States and Japan where recent regulatory changes have altered existing market links and have also enlarged markets because of competition in existing services modes or from inter-modal competition and the opening of markets to new services. Such changes lead to a redirection of marketing efforts by firms who have had close links to service providers and must now seek to widen their market since they no longer have an assured market, as well as by firms seeking to enter a market previously closed to them.

The interaction of changing service market structures on telecommunications equipment trade must not be viewed as being based solely on a monopoly/liberalisation debate, but rather by recognising that equipment trade may be stimulated, under certain conditions, without the need to change the basic framework of the regulatory regime. For example, trends in Europe towards the harmonization of norms may have important trade consequences within the European context. Other countries (e.g. the United States) view regional norms as creating protected markets and tend therefore to favour more world-wide standard making procedures. On the other hand, it needs to be recognised that regulatory changes in telecommunications services which are successful in one country may not be feasible in other countries depending on their size and business volume – the provision of some types of bypass services may be an example.

The increasing internationalisation of the world information technology industry through inter-firm ties and co-operation is affecting both the private communications service provision market, broadly defined, the telecommunications market and the telecommunications equipment industry and is playing an important role in reinforcing trade flows. This increased internationalisation of firms, both between equipment producers and equipment producers and users, is also an important factor in increased pressure for the opening of equipment and service markets on a competitive basis in Member countries.

Total OECD exports of telecommunications equipment increased at an annual average rate of 8.6 per cent between 1978 to 1985, from $5.1 billion to $9.0 billion – compared to the growth in manufacturing exports as a whole of 5.3 per cent annual average. OECD imports of telecommunications equipment from the world grew at an annual average rate of 16.0 per cent over 1978-1985 (from $2.3 billion to $6.5 billion) reflecting in particular the growth in imports of telephone line equipment and the high rate of growth in imports from the non-OECD area. Several countries experienced an absolute decline, in current dollars, in imports over the period.

The performance of the different OECD countries in telecommunications equipment exports differed considerably (Table 18). Countries such as Belgium and the Netherlands experienced absolute declines in telecommunications exports over the period or stagnant growth (Germany, Portugal, Spain); other countries, already in a strong position, continued to show strong growth (Canada, Japan and the United States). Yet other countries starting from a narrow base in telecommunications equipment exports showed a rapid growth in trade (Finland, Ireland), but exports often remain at a marginal level relative to consumption. Nevertheless exports of telecommunications equipment is highly concentrated with the top ten exporting countries supplying, on average during 1978-1985, 92 per cent of OECD exports, and the leading four countries – Japan, the United States, Germany and Sweden – 66 per cent of OECD telecommunications equipment exports.

The period 1978-1985 was characterised by considerable variations in the competitive positions of the major telecommunications producing and trading countries. Canada's competitive position showed a particularly strong increase. The export performance of Japan and the United States was also strong contrasting with the poor performance of Belgium, the Netherlands, Germany and Sweden. Four countries – Japan, the United States, Canada and France – were in fact responsible for 83 per cent of the increase in OECD export growth of telecommunications equipment, Japan alone accounting for 48 per cent of this increase. The sharp decline in the EEC's share of OECD reports on telecommunications is in particular evident. If intra-EEC exports are excluded, the EEC share of OECD telecommunications exports shows a decline from 44 per cent in 1978 to 29 per cent in 1984. Canada and Japan showed a significant increase in their relative specialisation in telecommunications exports, while in the case of Belgium, Germany, Italy, the Netherlands and the EEC, there was a deterioration in the relative importance of telecommunications exports in total manufacturing trade.

Telecommunications equipment trade balances are shown in Table 19 for OECD countries – eight OECD countries have had a continuous negative trade balance throughout 1978-1985 and eight countries a yearly positive trade balance throughout the period. Of the main equipment producing countries, only Canada had a deficit (in 1978 and 1979) and the United States which experienced a significant deterioration in its trade balance since 1983. Only Germany, Japan and Sweden have maintained a positive trade balance with the OECD over the 1978-85 period. The positive trade balances of the other countries have been mainly due to trade with the non-OECD area. The United States has had an increasingly large deficit in intra-OECD trade for line equipment – a deficit which increased sharply in 1982 as a result of deregulation. The United States deficit with the OECD doubled in 1983 combined with a significant reduction it its surplus with the non-OECD area, a surplus which had turned to a deficit by 1984. The table below indicates for selected products some details of the United States trade balance:

United States: Telecommunications Equipment Trade Balance for Selected Products
($ million)

	1982	1983	1984
Telephone switching equipment and parts	211.3	162.9	−154.8
Telephone instruments	−111.8	−387.4	−448.8
Other telephone equipment and parts	122.9	−119.4	−262.3
Teletype apparatus and parts	−74.3	−60.7	−117.9
Telegraph Apparatus and Parts	60.5	−8.2	−48.3
Cordless Handset Telephones	−107.4	−368.8	−259.6
Intercom Systems	−6.0	−6.6	−7.3
Telephone Answering Devices	−88.6	−112.5	−108.4

Source: U.S. Department of Commerce.

As the data show, approximately half of the United States deficit has resulted from customer premises equipment deficits rather than from carrier equipment.

In contrast to the United States, Japan has maintained a surplus in equipment trade with all major OECD producing countries although, with the exception of the United States, this surplus has been relatively small. The EEC as a whole has shown continued poor performance in trade with the OECD area maintaining a constant deficit in trade, although not high in value-terms. In contrast, the EEC has maintained throughout the 1978-84 period a healthy surplus in trade with the non-OECD area.

Two conclusions may be drawn from trade data. Firstly, that despite the proven competitiveness of Japanese firms as evidenced by their high penetration of the United States market, they have not been able to penetrate to any significant extent the more closed European markets. Secondly, despite being nurtured and protected, firms in the EEC have not made any significant inroads in open markets such as the United States where competitiveness is a much more important factor than in non-OECD markets. The fact that EEC firms have concentrated in non-OECD markets which are growing at slower rates than OECD markets has weakened their position.

The most important change which has occurred in trade of telecommunications equipment in the last few years is the significant growth in imports by the United States led largely by the deregulation of the telecommunications service market in 1982 (a compound rate of 44 per cent between 1982-85) and the counterpart to this growth – the important expansion in Japan's telecommunications exports. As yet, it is too early to ascertain whether a similar pattern will occur as a result of change in Japan's and the United Kingdom's regulatory framework. There are already indications that trade patterns will be affected at least to some degree: for example as noted in the previous section, in the United Kingdom orders have already been placed with non-United Kingdom companies for carrier equipment in contrast to the fact that over 95 per cent of British Telecom orders during 1973-83 were placed with British manufacturers.

Regulatory changes in the United States not only allowed for increased import competition, but by allowing AT&T Technologies to compete in equipment markets, have shifted the focus of United States firms toward export markets, particularly for switching equipment. Already several joint-ventures have been set up by American firms in equipment production aimed at facilitating market access. The longer term competitiveness of United States' firms competing more rigorously in their domestic markets against import competition as well as in export markets may become an important factor in changing the structural pattern of trade in telecommunications equipment.

An important principle of international trade is that of non-discrimination. The opening of the United States telecommunications equipment market has attracted many equipment manufacturers from other OECD countries because of its growth, size and ease of entry. However, the position of many of these firms in the United States market may become increasingly untenable politically in that they cannot expect to continue taking advantage of this market when a reciprocal opportunity does not exist for United States firms. This asymmetry in trade markets creates in particular difficulties since a domestic firm which has lost a domestic sale to a foreign firm cannot easily compensate for this loss by increasing exports.

The concern with trade has particularly clouded Japan-United States relations in view of the latter country's large deficit and small sales volume with Japan[24]. The completion of deregulation in 1985 in Japan, and the expectation that this may result in increased United States equipment sales, has shifted the focus of United States policy-makers to European markets and their restrictions. The Federal Communications Commission has initiated a Notice of Enquiry on whether it should restrict access to the United States market by countries that limit access to United States firms.

The discussion of exclusive bilateral market opening opportunities can fragment multilateral relations and can provide unfair advantage to firms of the countries participating in those bilateral negotiations – this is especially the case when the basis of negotiations centres around bilateral trade balance. The fact that the European Commission has not participated in the extension of the GATT Procurement code as regards PTT procurement puts it in an uncomfortable position given that it is not in a position to complain about discriminatory access to markets.

Recent legislative initiatives in the United States regarding telecommunications trade legislation aim to open foreign equipment markets and service markets, firstly through negotiation, and if this does not succeed, through retaliatory action.

The market structure of telecommunications equipment in a country and the trade pattern for this equipment directly reflect the requirement to meet service demands and is consequently dependent on the structure of the telecommunications service framework. This does not imply that direct trade instruments are not important, however it needs stressing that many of the issues which become apparent in trade are often not trade policy based but derive from regulatory policy and need to be understood in the context of the telecommunications service framework.

5. Protection of Equipment Markets

Protection of the equipment industry has been undertaken by most countries through the use of procurement practices, standards procedures and type approval procedures.

The manufacture of telephone exchange systems is viewed by many countries as strategic and thus requiring protection. There is however seldom any attempt to allocate priorities between competing ends. Thus if the goal is an effective and efficient telephone system then as long as equipment meets technical requirements it should be used. Imports in this case provide more effective competition than a second domestic company. If the goal is to obtain an equipment producing industry which is competitive internationally then protection of the domestic industry will not attain the desired results.

A concern in all equipment producing countries, including the United States, is that free trade in equipment – particularly large central office switches – could have long-term implications vis-a-vis their technological position in information technology. Such industrial policy considerations should not distort telecommunications policy. The close synergy existing between the service and equipment sector implies that the R&D know-how is unlikely to weaken because of competitive trade. Further, many major non-equipment producing carriers already undertake their own R&D (NTT, DGT, Deutsche Bundespost). Trade on the contrary tends to sharpen firms ability to innovate. In addition, there are more direct means of ensuring adequate research. For example, the Director General of Telecommunications in the United Kingdom has suggested that[25]:

> "One way of resolving this problem might be to establish a UK research organisation which would be given the objective of maintaining a competence in modern switching technology, which would be financed by firms in the industry, and which would have the obligation of making its know-how available to UK firms on an even-handed basis".

Further concerns, as noted previously, revolve around the competitive ability of firms.

The longer-term adjustment costs of continued closed equipment markets and government procurement policies will be more severe and abrupt than a commitment to phase-in liberalisation. Procurement has not only involved the direct purchase of central office switches by telecommunications administrations, but has included the supply of terminal equipment directly by these administrations.

Standards and Type-Approval

The information technology industries, and in particular telecommunications, depend for their efficient functioning on interaction between equipment, which in turn requires that such equipment is compatible. The requirement for interoperability of information technology systems is increasing in importance with the widespread diffusion of such systems in the service sector and on the factory floor. The increasing trend towards electronic interlinkage between systems means that compatibility has become a key constraint. In terms of economic efficiency the "existence of interfacing standards and their quality determines how far investments in communications infrastructure can be optimised"[26].

Standards and standard-setting are a two-edged policy instrument. Their potential adverse influence has long been recognised and used effectively, in conjunction with homologation/type approval procedures, to close equipment markets to foreign competition. In turn the importance of standards in unifying markets is shown by efforts of the CCITT to achieve worldwide service markets. The recognition of the importance of standards in unifying markets has been the basis of recent EC initiatives to achieve open and competitive markets throughout the Community. The recent agreement by France, Germany, Italy and the United Kingdom on standards and specifications for a joint mobile telephone system to be set-up by 1991 is an example of an area where without such agreement on standards, splintered markets would result in inefficiencies in equipment and service provision.

Efforts by the CCITT to achieve worldwide standards for digital communications and ISDN have had de facto support from all OECD countries. However, several countries view the standard-making process as the outcome of the dynamics of competition and are therefore concerned that "prior" standardization may impair competition.

Nevertheless, in recent years changing business attitudes – especially in the United States – have recognised the need to develop and apply common standards. This recognition is based partly on the fact that standards have become a major impediment to growth. Thus recent business initatives to co-operate on standards all take as their basis Open Systems Interconnection Standards supported by the ISO and CCITT[27].

All countries have constraints and approval procedures for terminal equipment connected to public networks which vary from monopoly provision of equipment by PTTs to liberalised provision of equipment based on minimum technical standards and on self-certification. For the business sector a high priority regarding type-approval is for mutual acceptance of test results by foreign countries in order to eliminate repetitive and costly testing procedures. Costs and impediments in obtaining approval can be a serious constraint to firms in carrying out their day-to-day operations.

Recent trends in separating type-approval authority from telecommunications administrations is accelerating type-approval, and by introducing mutual recognition procedures, improved liberalisation in equipment trade can be expected. In Europe, for example, co-ordination of the European Community and EFTA countries (through the Conférence Européene des Administrations, des Postes et Télécommunications) is leading to mutual recognition of type-approval for terminal equipment and promoting certification centres in Europe[28].

Changes facilitating market entry have also occurred in Japan with the liberalisation of telecommunications. These have included a reduction in the number of standards for terminal equipment, acceleration of approval procedures, self-certification and neutrality by setting up a Designated Approval Agency.

6. Research and Development

The impact of technology on equipment and new systems is having widespread effects on telecommunications services from two perspectives. Firstly, in terms of existing services, technology has enhanced the performance and capabilitites of existing systems and widened their service range. Secondly, technology has led to a range of alternate ways to provide those services[29].

Previous sections have already noted the importance of technology in structural change and in forcing regulatory change. The impact of technology on telecommunications market structures has had differential effects. In the case of innovations affecting production of equipment the impact has been towards concentration, especially as a result of high and increasing R&D costs and with production technologies which have tended to be "streamlining". Some technologies have served to weaken the PTT monopoly base while others have potentially enhanced it. ISDN, as previously suggested, could allow PTTs, as the network operator, to control transmission flows for all types of information. Similarly, developments such as Software Defined Networks, whereby the dedicated leasing of lines could be replaced by ISDN overcoming issues related to leased line capacity, could be used to strenghthen the PTT's position.

The role of government in R&D directly in terms of expenditures on information technology, and indirectly, through telecommunications administrations has been important. The European Community in recent years has undertaken important initiatives in communications R&D (e.g. in EUREKA, ESPRIT, RACE) where the aim is not only to ensure that European industries are at the forefront of technology, but also to ensure that in the longer-run communications markets and services in Europe are compatible and integrated.

The importance of communications R&D rests on the wide range of technologies covered such as microelectronics, digital switching, transmission technologies, optoelectronics, software, signal processing, and artificial intelligence. Much of the technology is transferable to other activities in information technology: for example transmission technology based on fibre-optics will be important in factory automation both on the factory floor and in creating plant information networks.

There has been a tendency too to overestimate the rate of change of technology and in particular its likely impact. The lag from invention to productive use is invariably relatively long as illustrated by fibre-optic technology[30]:

1966	–	The technology emerged;
1970	–	First optical fibre achieving required pulse strength for use in telephone systems;
1975-76	–	Field tests using fibre-optic transmission began.

However, once a technology has proved cost-effective and reliable, diffusion is very rapid but uneven. This has been the case for fibre-optics where industry utilisation rates have increased significantly. In addition, diffusion has also stimulated further innovations (e.g. in the case of fibre-optics a significant reduction in repeater spacing has been achieved within a relatively short-time frame).

NOTES AND REFERENCES

1. Good data on market size do not exist and it is difficult to reconcile various data made available by market consultancy companies. Often a different coverage is used to define the equipment industry, different sources and different exchange rates. Official statistics do not provide market data. It is also increasingly difficult to refer to a homogeneous group of "telecommunications equipment" and to differentiate between network equipment, data communications equipment and office automation equipment.

2. For example, Electronics (McGraw-Hill) of the 24th June 1985 estimates the market at $75 billion, A.D. Little (WTIP) at $79.5 billion.

3. Exclusion from the world market was total for Western Electric (AT&T) by legal constraints until 1st January 1984. The seven BOCs are presently constrained from equipment production.

4. For the OECD as a whole telecommunications export credits as a percentage of total telecommunications exports to non-OECD markets were 25.5 per cent in 1983 and 17.7 per cent in 1981.

5. The proportion of PTT investment construction expenditure on switching equipment is illustrated by the following data:

	1974	1983	1984	1985
	%	%	%	%
Canada	–	38.3	34.0	–
Germany (1976)	26.2	26.6	23.0	20.1
Netherlands	49.8	38.7	42.0	32.9
Spain	38.9	27.9	23.7	20.7
Sweden	27.4	18.5	16.3	–
France	25.8	26.4	22.7	–

Source: ITU.

6. AT&T, GTE in the United States; NEC, Hitachi, Fujitsu in Japan; Plessey (and its U.S. subsidiary Stromberg-Carlson) and GEC in the United Kingdom; Ericsson in Sweden; Northern Telecom in Canada; CGE and CGCT in France; Siemens in Germany; Italtel in Italy; Telenokia in Finland; and Alcatel the joint-venture formed at the beginning of 1987 from the telecommunications interests of ITT and CGE involving ITT telecommunications subsidiaries based in several European countries. Several other companies exist as well but of a smaller size.

7. Ericsson claims to have invested 10 million man-hours in the software for the AXE digital switching system (Ericsson, "Digital Telecommunications : The Welcome Revolution").

8. Siemens reportedly spent $200 million to adapt its EWS-D switch for the United States market. Similarly, ITT's expenditure to try and adapt its System 12 switch for this market reportedly reached $150 million, representing about 15 per cent of original development costs, before abandoning its efforts. Ericsson spent approximately $60 million to adapt AXE to the U.S. market.

9. U.S. Industrial Outlook 1985.

10. Ibid.

11. The FCC Carterfone decision of 1968 gave permission to connect privately supplied subscriber apparatus to AT&T's network, but complete freedom for interconnection was achieved only in 1977 when telephone company connection boxes were declared unnecessary.

12. Such adjustments have already affected the United States production structure. For example in 1985 AT&T shifted production of consumer telephone equipment to Singapore.

13. Despite deregulation the United States' government still has influence over communications service, and through procurement, on equipment, by virtue of the size of its contracts. In particular, the General Services Administration contract to set up and manage the U.S. government's all-digital network will have a considerable impact on the industry.

14. Several legislative initiatives in the United States Congress on telecommunications are stressing the requirement for reciprocity and recent initiatives by the Federal Communications Commission appear to be also taking such an approach. For example, in late 1986 the FCC adopted a notice of inquiry and proposed rule-making aimed at developing a model for regulation of telecommunications goods and services and determining what steps the Commission might take to limit access to United States markets by providers of telecommunications goods and services from countries whose markets are found to be closed to entry by United States providers.

15. Based on the U.S.-Japan bilateral agreement, NTT began procurement of material from the U.S. in January 1981 when procurement was 3.2 billion yen ($14.5 million). At the end of fiscal 1985 NTT equipment procurement from abroad amounted to 37 billion yen ($155.8 million) of which about 90 per cent was sourced from the United States.

16. The United States subsidiary of Northern Telecom is the exception.

17. The Council of the European Communities agreed in 1984 that Members should open 10 per cent of their equipment markets by volume to transmission and switching procurement from other Members of the Community on an *experimental* basis; it was also agreed that for telematics terminals markets should be completely open.

18. The need to avoid duplicative research has received recognition by firms and policy-makers in the EEC, leading to ESPRIT and RACE and to co-operation between firms, e.g. by CIT-Alcatel, Italtel, Plessey and Siemens in R & D for ISDN.

19. Office of Telecommunications (U.K.), British Telecom's procurement of Digital Exchanges, July 1985. Oftel argued that a loss of 250 000 lines bringing output down to 1 million lines could increase average cost of production per line by about 10 per cent.

20. The setting-up of production facilities in foreign markets is not necessarily effective in terms of achieving the required scale economies even though this may help recuperate R & D expenses.

21. In 1982 Thomson-Brandt was also nationalised. The recent acquisition of the assets for public telecommunications equipment of Alcatel-Thomson by CGE has effectively left the DGT with only one company from which to purchase central switching equipment. CGCT, which is financially weak, has only 16 per cent of the French switch market.

22. The PBX market share in the United States measured by installed lines has changed rapidly:

	1980	1985
AT&T	76.0%	49%
Rolm	6.6	12
N.Telecom	5.3	11
Mitel	1.7	9
GTE	2.7	5

Source: Yankee Group.

23. National Telecommunications and Information Administration, US Department of Commerce, NTIA Competition Benefits Report, p. 7, 8th November 1985.

24. The trade deficit of the United States with Japan and concern that restrictive trade measures may be imposed, has led many Japanese companies to set up production facilities in the United States. (For example, NEC and Fujitsu have been producing mobile telephone equipment in the U.S. and Oki has transformed its operations from local assembly to an integrated local production. Matsushita will produce facsimile equipment in addition to its key set production facilities.)

25. OFTEL, British Telecom's Procurement of Digital Exchanges, London, July 1985.

26. For an overview of standardization issues see: OECD, Standards in Information and Communications Technology, 1987.

27. The Corporation for Open Systems set-up in the United States in 1986 by 18 leading computer companies will co-operate in selecting standards and certifying products. In 1984 General Motors originated the Manufacturing Automation Protocol, and in 1985 Boeing, the Technical and Office Protocols, both committed to OSI. In Europe the Standards Promotion and Awareness Group, an association of aerospace and computer companies is also committed to OSI. Similarly the Communications Networking for Manufacturing Applications association in Europe formed in 1986 by users and equipment producers will be based on OSI. All the above initiatives have implications for communications standards.

28. The European Community Directive 86/361/EEC on the Mutual Acceptance of Test Results comes into force on 9th June 1987.

29. For example, for some services a local-area network, or a PBX system can be used.

30. United States Department of Commerce. It is worth recalling that the telephone required about 70 years to attain a penetration rate of 50 per cent of households in the United States.

Chapter V

CONCLUSIONS

The communications equipment and service industries have over the past several years become crucial to the major OECD countries. The industry provides the transportation infrastructure and networks for a range of new industries, it plays an important role in influencing the structure and activity of other key manufacturing and service industries and it is increasingly a major factor in the competitive advantage in user industries. The changes in telecommunications are not limited to telephony or business services but have spilled over into areas where telecommunications has traditionally played a minor role such as factory and office automation.

The previous analysis has shown the growing role of telecommunications services in GDP, its importance in investment and the role of equipment production and exports. The increasing dependence of key economic sectors on communications technology merits stressing. The rate of diffusion of communications technology, equipment and services across sectors and the ability to utilise these efficiently are dependent to a large extent on the telecommunications service market structure and regulations related to these structures. Adjustment in telecommunications policy can play an important role in facilitating the adjustment and restructuring of other markets and economic sectors.

In reviewing changes which have occurred in telecommunications service structures in the OECD one factor stands out. That is the reluctance of many countries to take decisive action to enhance the efficiency of their economic structure and open new opportunities to industries by adjusting telecommunications structures. Experience has shown that hesitation will in many cases weaken industrial structure and performance, as well as innovative ability, eventually requiring extra efforts to catch-up, but seldom surpassing, major competitors. In addition, catch-up policies are often linked with increased protectionism. The danger that this could occur again is apparent as OECD economies shift to information-based economic structures where efficient communications networks, know-how and services are beginning to play a major role.

At the national level there has been a lack of awareness of the economic importance of telecommunications policy – its macroeconomic and microeconomic importance. As a result telecommunications policy making has often been left with bodies which have a vested interest to maintain the status quo or at least to slow change. The policy logic of curtailing investment opportunities and employment creation in communications-related service areas through restrictive competition policies, needs to be strongly questioned. The fault has not rested solely with telecommunications administrations, but also with government economic policy which in certain countries subjected telecommunications administrations to financial and other restrictions, retarding the efficient provision of services.

The debate as to the extent to which economic efficiency criteria should govern telecommunications policy rather than social objectives continues in most OECD countries. The two objectives are not mutually exclusive and should not be viewed as extremes of a spectrum. Debate needs also to avoid raising deteriorating universal service conditions as a spectre justifying policy immobility.

Thus, the commitment to the provision of universal telecommunications services must not be confounded with competition. The two concepts are not necessarily in confrontation. Neither does a commitment to liberalisation in telecommunications imply complete deregulation, but rather a commitment to allow competition and encourage it to the degree possible with the minimum of regulation to safeguard competition itself and to safeguard the quality and universality of service, and other social objectives with which the provision of telecommunications services might be burdened.

In this regard the emergence of competition in telecommunications services is clearly proving to be a challenge to telecommunications administrations. It is difficult to maintain the fine line between the societal benefits of economic efficiency brought about by competition, and societal benefits in ensuring that the standard of service, pricing and universal service provision are maintained in the public interest. Maintaining such a balance can usually be achieved more easily through an independent regulatory body.

Arguments used by telecommunications administrations in justifying the monopoly provision of services are increasingly being brought into question. Technological changes have altered cost and supply characteristics. It has become increasingly evident that network size is not highly related with cost and efficiency and that for a whole range of new services, user needs require differentiated rather than homogeneous services.

The international consensus which existed in telecommunications in the past, based on similar service structures is being rapidly fragmented by the policy and structural changes in several key economies which are on the threshold of maximising the benefits they can reap from new telecommunications technologies. Longer-term international structural problems may arise from differences between countries which have successfully transformed their structures to an information-economy basis and lagging countries which have delayed the transformation process. These structural differences could tend to promote protectionism and create trade problems in the equipment and service areas.

At the international level, the difficulty in trying to compartmentalise and place within treaty provisions a changing and dynamic technology whose implications are becoming more widespread, is also challenging this international consensus. Efforts to bring telecommunications services within the sphere of trade instruments will also be a policy challenge which needs to be met over the next few years.

The aim of telecommunications policy should be to serve the customer, offer the customer a wide choice, ensure that network operations are disciplined by the market and ensure that competition in the provision of equipment is not distorted by burdensome and unnecessarily restrictive regulations. In terms of these goals, the present regulatory framework in many countries is not in line with market requirements and not keeping pace with technological change. Certainly such frameworks do not reflect the significant adjustments which have taken place in equipment markets and performance and service markets and potentials. The inadequacy of the telecommunications policy review process in many countries needs to be mentioned in this regard.

There is a requirement for more analytical work in terms of the economy-wide benefits and costs of present telecommunications regulatory policies in many Member countries, which stress in particular the impact of such policies on the growth and development of other economic sectors. This would allow policy makers to obtain a clearer understanding of the economic role of telecommunications in economies and how this role is changing. An era of adjustment has begun in telecommunications – it is important that countries take the opportunity now to adjust their telecommunications structures in order to ensure a smooth transition path and to take full advantage of the information technology revolution.

Annex I

STATISTICAL TABLES

Table 1. Total income from all telecommunications services as a percentage of GDP

(Based on national currency and current prices)

	1974	1980	1983	1984	1985	Growth in ratio 1974-85
Australia	1.35	1.66	1.92	2.01	2.05	3.88
Austria	1.02	1.52	1.65	1.68	1.70	4.81
Belgium	0.83	1.09	1.21	1.31	1.33	4.38
Canada	1.77	2.02	2.36	2.34	2.34	2.60
Denmark	1.22	1.18	1.31	1.37	1.54	2.17
Finland	1.24	1.58	1.59	1.51	1.51	1.83
France	1.13	1.68	1.71	1.87	2.10	5.78
Germany	1.78	1.76	1.80	1.82	1.83	0.24
Greece	1.39	1.37	1.78	1.70	1.67	1.65
Iceland	1.32	1.31	1.62	–	1.98	3.76
Ireland	1.07	1.75	2.32	2.29	2.59	8.31
Italy	1.18	1.29	1.57	1.68	1.76	3.74
Japan	1.45	1.66	1.61	1.59	1.59	0.72
Luxembourg	0.95	1.61	1.88	1.59	1.56	4.60
Netherlands	1.28	1.37	1.45	1.48	1.54	1.71
New Zealand	–	2.02	2.33	2.24	2.19	4.15[3]
Norway	1.57	1.47	1.96	1.97	2.01	2.25
Portugal	1.13	1.84	2.48	2.97	3.16	9.77
Spain	0.91	1.24	1.45	1.50	1.52	4.75
Sweden	1.52	1.40	1.59	1.71	1.84	1.77
Switzerland	1.68	2.07	2.07	2.20	2.23	2.65
Turkey	0.44	0.62[1]	0.69[2]	1.06	1.32	10.54
United Kingdom	1.65	1.55	2.12	2.15	2.18	2.58
United States	2.00	2.12	2.28	2.87	2.84	3.24

Source: ITU for Income Data. OECD for GDP.
1. 1979.
2. 1982.
3. 1985/1980.

Table 2. Telecommunications investment[1] as share of gross fixed capital formation
(Based on national currency and current prices)

| | 1974 | 1975 | 1980 | 1983 | 1984 | 1985 | Growth in ratio | |
							1985/74	1985/80
Australia	3.4	3.2	2.6	3.4	2.7	2.7	−2.0	0.6
Austria	2.2	2.7	2.3	3.2	3.5	3.6	4.6	8.8
Belgium	2.3	2.7	2.2	2.9	3.1	2.8	1.7	4.9
Canada	4.2	4.0	3.5	3.1	3.1	2.8	−3.7	−4.7
Denmark	2.1	2.5	2.7	2.4	2.2	2.1	0.2	−4.9
Finland	2.2	2.4	2.0	2.0	2.0	2.3	0.4	3.4
France	1.9	3.0	3.6	3.3	3.3	3.1	4.7	−2.9
Germany	−	2.2	2.8	3.3	3.6	4.1	6.5	8.1
Greece	3.2	2.8	2.1	4.1	4.2	3.4	0.7	9.8
Iceland	1.1	1.1	1.1	1.3	1.8	1.6	3.5	4.8
Ireland	3.1	4.8	3.8	5.5	−	3.8	1.7	0.0
Italy	3.7	4.5	3.6	4.6	4.4	4.3	1.3	3.3
Japan	−	2.4	1.9	1.9	1.8	1.8	−3.0	−1.6
Luxembourg	2.0	1.6	1.9	−	1.0	1.4	−3.1	−5.9
Netherlands	1.8	2.0	1.9	1.7	1.6	2.0	1.3	1.5
New Zealand	−	−	0.8	1.6	2.4	2.2	−	20.8
Norway	2.1	2.0	3.0	2.6	2.4	2.8	2.5	−1.5
Portugal	2.4	2.7	1.7	2.6	3.0	3.4	3.4	14.9
Spain	4.0	4.2	3.4	3.4	3.6	3.4	−1.5	0.2
Sweden	1.5	1.3	1.7	3.3	3.1	2.9	6.2	11.8
Switzerland	3.1	3.4	2.6	2.9	2.8	2.9	−0.7	2.8
Turkey	1.3	1.7	0.6	2.8	3.5	4.3	11.3	46.3
United Kingdom	−	3.2	−	2.7	3.1	2.9	−1.0	−
United States	4.0	3.6	3.7	2.8	2.4	2.9	−3.1	−4.9

Source: ITU − telecommunications investment. OECD − Gross Fixed Capital Formation.
1. Excludes investment in land and buildings.

Table 3. **Telephone main lines per 100 inhabitants**
(Ranked on the basis of 1985 data)

	1974	1980	1983	1984	1985	Growth 1974-1984 %
Sweden (5)*	49.71	58.00	60.24	61.51	62.78	2.1
United States (2)	36.82	41.43	47.27	48.17	50.57	2.9
Switzerland (1)	37.01	44.46	47.75	48.95	50.18	2.8
Denmark (6)	31.71	43.43	46.98	48.24	49.74	4.2
Canada (4)	35.27	41.44	41.90	45.34	49.18	2.3
Finland (8)	26.45	36.40	41.62	43.08	44.68	4.9
Iceland (12)	32.56	37.28	39.66	40.42	42.39	2.4
Luxembourg (15)	28.49	36.26	37.98	40.16	42.08	3.6
Germany (7)	19.61	33.35	38.34	40.22	41.94	7.2
France (11)	11.81	29.95	38.26	40.20	41.75	12.2
Norway (3)	21.66	28.65	36.77	39.07	41.37	6.1
Australia (9)	24.49	32.28	37.01	38.81	40.38	4.7
Netherlands (13)	22.62	34.57	38.02	39.12	40.20	5.4
New Zealand (18)	31.01	35.08	37.14	37.63	39.80	2.3
Japan (10)	26.53	33.06	35.58	36.50	37.57	3.2
United Kingdom (17)	22.87	31.44	34.68	35.75	36.95	4.5
Austria (14)	18.29	29.02	33.75	34.97	36.12	6.4
Belgium (16)	18.08	25.01	28.85	29.94	31.05	5.0
Italy (19)	16.49	23.07	27.45	28.99	30.45	5.7
Greece (22)	17.55	23.54	27.56	29.57	30.15	5.0
Spain (21)	12.11	19.34	22.15	23.14	24.20	6.5
Ireland (20)	9.80	14.20	17.47	18.93	19.74	6.6
Portugal (23)	8.00	10.07	12.42	13.08	13.75	5.0
Turkey (24)	1.52	2.46	3.50	3.98	4.51	10.4
OECD Average:	24.77	32.00	36.39	37.57	39.23	4.3
EEC–10	18.27	29.50	34.44	36.00	37.41	6.7

Source: International Telecommunications Union, Yearbook of Common Carrier Telecommunications Statistics (11th edition) and PTT Annual Reports.
* Bracketed numbers represent OECD ranking of countries in terms of Gross Domestic Product at market prices per capita at current U.S.$ for 1983.

Table 4. Telephone sets per 100 inhabitants

	1974	1980	1983	1984	1985	Growth 1974-1985*
Sweden	63.46	79.67	88.97	–	–	3.8
Switzerland	58.67	72.23	78.88	81.00	83.25	3.2
United States	67.32	79.22	75.12	75.10	85.67	3.2
Denmark	42.89	64.06	71.88	74.88	78.33	5.6
Canada	55.61	68.68	66.73	65.00	63.00	2.0
New Zealand	47.64	55.03	60.11	61.72	64.72	2.8
Norway	34.18	46.02	58.02	62.28	–	6.2
Netherlands	34.60	51.99	57.58	59.23	61.03	5.3
Germany	30.24	46.38	57.20	59.80	62.11	6.8
Finland	35.79	49.67	57.19	59.38	61.78	5.1
Luxembourg	39.66	54.67	54.92	–	–	3.0
France	23.65	46.83	57.53	60.06	62.27	9.2
Australia	36.44	48.68	53.96	53.54	55.40	3.9
United Kingdom	36.38	47.33	51.55	52,26	–	3.7
Iceland	40.46	47.81	52.74	–	–	2.9
Japan	34.43	45.92	51.32	53.30	55.18	4.4
Austria	26.15	39.87	45.95	47.60	49.24	5.9
Belgium	27.29	36.92	41.70	43.05	44.09	4.5
Italy	24.85	34.17	40.46	42.70	44.84	5.6
Spain	20.04	31.68	34.96	36.01	36.94	5.7
Greece	20.78	29.00	33.64	35.66	37.40	5.5
Ireland	12.61	19.11	23.49	–	26.45	7.0
Portugal	11.34	13.96	16.83	17.48	18.03	4.3
Turkey	2.28	3.91	5.57	6.33	6.93	10.6
Total OECD:	40.44	52.62	55.48	56.61	60.95	3.8
EEC (10)	28.87	43.45	51.05	53.04	55.05	6.0

Source: ITU.
* Or to latest year available.

Table 5. **Telephones per 100 population (1983): selected cities**

Canada	Ottawa	84
	Sherbrooke	58
United States	Washington D.C.	173
	New York	74
	Albuquerque, NM	40
Austria	Vienna	73
	Graz	61
Belgium	Brussels	76
	Antwerp	53
	Aalst	35
Denmark	Copenhagen	97
	Esbjerg	67
Finland	Helsinki	98
	Vantaa	45
France	Paris	102
	Marseille	61
Germany	Bonn	85
	Hamburg	94
Greece	Athens	52
	Volos	26
Ireland	Dublin	34
	Limerick	36
Italy	Milan	74
	Naples	35
Norway	Oslo	97
	Sandnes	46
Portugal	Lisbon	55
	Braga	12
Spain	Madrid	59
	Cordoba	35
Sweden	Stockholm	133
	Skelleftea	79
Switzerland	Berne	98
	Aarau	74
United Kingdom	London	75
	Wolverhampton	53
New Zealand	Wellington	84
	Auckland	69
Japan	Tokyo	85
	Hitachi	48

Source: The World's Telephones, AT&T, 1983.

Table 6. **Waiting list for telephone main lines as ratio of total main lines**

	1974	1980	1983	1984	1985
Australia (A)	0.65	0.22	0.88	0.10	0.12
Austria (A)	13.81	6.71	2.36	1.74	1.47
Belgium (A)	1.25	1.54	0.58	0.30	0.23
Canada	0.00	0.00	0.00	0.00	0.00
Denmark	0.08	0.02	0.00	0.00	0.00
Finland	0.00	0.08	0.05	0.07	0.07
France	15.27	3.52	0.50	0.26	0.16
Germany (B)	0.70	0.42	0.14	0.17	0.11
Greece (B)	15.96	35.15	33.20	31.89	0.00
Iceland	0.00	0.00	0.00	0.00	0.00
Ireland	13.73	18.63	9.79	6.16	3.94
Italy (B)	4.43	6.36	3.08	2.41	1.90
Japan	0.00	0.30	0.26	0.24	0.17
Luxembourg	6.86	1.52	1.41	1.32	1.32
Netherlands	1.43	1.66	0.84	0.82	0.94
New Zealand	0.96	0.70	0.13	0.19	0.23
Norway	4.17	7.08	0.83	0.05	0.05
Portugal	17.10	12.50	9.56	6.55	3.16
Spain	14.50	7.37	3.50	3.01	2.71
Sweden	0.00	0.00	0.00	0.00	0.00
Switzerland (A)	0.79	0.18	0.13	0.12	0.13
Turkey	112.85	140.57	109.10	94.85	80.90
United Kingdom (C)	0.00	1.49	0.02	0.00	0.00
United States	0.06	0.07	0.00	0.00	0.00

Source: ITU Yearbook.
Note: The waiting list consists of applications for connection which cannot be completed owing to lack of technical infrastructure (equipment, lines, etc.)
For each country the definition differs as to period, e.g. for Australia it comprises applications for subscriptions which cannot be completed within 3 months, in Germany the period is 4 weeks.
A = 3 months, B = 4 weeks, C = 8 weeks.

Table 7. **Total income from telecommunications services**
(Millions of constant U.S. dollars at exchange rates and price levels of 1980)

	1974	1985	Growth 1985/74	$ per capita		
				1974	1985	Growth 1985/74
Australia	1 827.03	3 615.55	6.40	133.14	229.53	5.07
Austria	662.20	1 415.72	7.15	87.14	187.38	7.20
Belgium	859.71	1621.00	5.93	88.01	164.45	5.84
Canada	3 738.66	6 999.49	5.87	166.94	275.79	4.66
Denmark	719.78	1 144.05	4.30	142.67	223.75	4.17
Finland	540.07	888.79	4.63	115.13	181.35	4.21
France	6 311.45	14 571.96	7.90	120.31	264.16	7.41
Germany	12 510.83	15 866.54	2.18	201.61	260.04	2.34
Greece	426.16	702.04	4.64	47.55	70.55	3.65
Iceland	–	–	–	–	–	–
Ireland	159.60	543.09	11.78	51.09	152.46	10.45
Italy	4 006.18	7 307.12	5.62	72.67	127.90	5.27
Japan	10 859.93	20 083.42	5.75	98.59	166.31	4.86
Luxembourg	40.60	79.96	6.35	114.38	218.46	6.05
Netherlands	1 902.14	2 692.16	3.21	140.43	185.87	2.58
New Zealand	0.00	575.93	–	0.00	176.99	–
Norway	688.40	1 350.34	6.32	172.75	325.54	5.92
Portugal	229.39	833.51	12.44	25.21	81.87	11.30
Spain	1 738.96	3 457.48	6.45	49.48	89.56	5.54
Sweden	1 722.14	2 501.40	3.45	211.05	299.56	3.23
Switzerland	1 689.15	2 427.03	3.35	261.48	371.67	3.24
Turkey	191.87	956.92	15.73	4.87	19.18	13.27
United Kingdom	0.00	12 804.08	–	0.00	226.14	–
United States	46 201.59	86 134.45	5.83	216.04	359.96	4.75
Total OECD	100 089.78	188 638.14	5.93	134.42	233.44	5.14
EEC (10)	26 936.45	57 332.01	7.11	101.01	209.81	6.81

Sources: ITU for Income Data. OECD for exchange rates, and GDP price index, and population.

Table 8. **Telephone traffic**[1]

	Growth in traffic		Per capita traffic (calls per person)			
	$\frac{1983}{1974}$	$\frac{1983}{1978}$	1974	1978	1983	1984
Australia	7.0	7.8	267	324	440	474
Austria	5.0	4.7	2 287	2 838	3 556	3 322
Belgium	5.4[2]	6.8[2]	143	171	194	–
Canada	4.0	4.1	926	1 026	1 186	–
Denmark	4.9	3.5	454	582	690	696
Finland	–	7.2[3]	–	310[3]	402	447
France (*)	12.2	9.8	493	855	1 335	1 436
Germany	6.9	7.5	224	289	414	432
Greece	–	11.3		297	486	549
Iceland	–	–	–	–	–	–
Ireland (*)	14.2[2]	19.5[2]	233	341	460	–
Italy	5.1	5.1	180	215	272	305
Japan	–	–	–	–	–	–
Luxembourg	–	–	–	–	–	–
Netherlands	5.9	5.2	243	307	385	400
New Zealand	24.8[4]	46.1	25.7	27.54	178.4	190
Norway	–	–	–	–	–	–
Portugal	–	–	–	–	–	–
Spain	–	–	–	–	–	–
Sweden (*)	4.7	4.1	2 083	2 540	3 091	3 237
Switzerland	3.1	5.2	1 287	1 334	1 678	1 718
Turkey	–	–	–	–	–	–
United Kingdom	4.6	4.4	255	309	382	407
United States	6.0	6.1	1 055	1 272	1 622	1 508

Source: ITU.
1. Based on number of calls with exception for countries marked with an asterisk where number of charged pulses is used. For New Zealand and Austria traffic is measured by charged minutes.
2. 1980.
3. 1979.
4. 1975.

Table 9. **Income from calls as percentage of total telecommunications income**

(on basis of national currency at current prices)

	1974	1978	1983	1985
Australia	60.6	58.9	55.3	55.2
Austria	71.0	70.7	65.2	64.0
Belgium	62.8	58.1	56.9	53.5
Canada[1]	93.2	94.6	93.7	–
Denmark	50.1	51.4	46.4	46.1
Finland	60.4	64.9	59.3	55.8
France	59.4	58.6	64.1	61.8
Germany	54.5	55.6	57.5	58.0
Greece	70.7	73.7	77.4	77.6
Iceland[1]	50.7	48.1	48.7	52.0
Ireland	70.7	69.9	68.6	–
Italy	70.0	67.0	64.6	63.1
Japan	65.8	61.8	59.8	–
Luxembourg	68.1	61.4	65.3[2]	66.5
Netherlands	45.2	41.5	41.3	40.9
New Zealand	–	37.0[3]	40.0	40.1
Norway	62.9	63.8	60.0	62.2
Portugal	62.4	50.8	53.8	51.3
Spain	55.2	58.9	59.2	54.2
Sweden	63.1	60.3	52.1	51.5
Switzerland	50.8	59.5	60.5	60.2
Turkey	72.7	73.5	63.4[2]	60.8
United Kingdom	51.2	59.0	56.8[2]	53.9
United States	46.6	49.8	50.8	58.8

Source: ITU.
1. Total income from the telephone service used instead of income from calls
2. 1982.
3. 1979.

Table 10. **Investment by common carriers: 3-year moving average**
(Millions of US$ in 1980 prices & exchange rates)

	1975-77	1977-79	1979-81	1981-83	1983-85
Australia	1 068.69	1 137.05	2 783.07	4 688.73	1 168.93
Austria	475.34	463.43	485.39	552.91	626.89
Belgium	592.90	542.88	528.74	569.96	585.55
Canada	1 953.13	1 954.56	2 142.45	1 957.15	1 838.45
Denmark	338.52	344.07	321.15	276.34	273.63
Finland	327.54	290.42	266.22	285.79	306.81
France	4 521.95	5 598.16	5 190.54	4 566.97	4 535.04
Germany	3 602.34	3 996.53	5 091.22	5 649.56	6 337.29
Greece	190.12	185.87	239.99	323.36	324.52
Iceland	769.64	839.91	621.35	8.99	11.85
Ireland	154.09	145.82	221.08	311.92	157.60
Italy	3 155.88	3 133.05	2 798.39	3 013.77	3 355.02
Japan	6 529.62	6 822.20	6 637.91	6 646.38	6 753.59
Luxembourg	19.97	23.34	15.27	9.46	11.26
Netherlands	675.37	691.08	625.38	534.61	576.18
New Zealand	0.00	22.72	55.73	76.21	124.90
Norway	343.68	427.57	427.98	407.03	406.29
Portugal	129.79	123.95	144.02	171.56	184.65
Spain	1 975.81	1 814.47	1 611.98	1 535.91	1 497.34
Sweden	305.00	298.10	497.74	779.98	776.75
Switzerland	716.99	657.79	636.60	702.87	764.39
Turkey	221.00	185.45	52.31	114.10	472.60
United Kingdom	2 967.63	2 494.53	2 746.40	2 837.55	2 792.07
United States	15 557.65	17 927.97	18 683.32	16 523.22	15 984.57
OECD:	46 592.66	50 120.91	52 824.24	52 544.34	49 866.16
EEC (10)	16 218.77	17 155.32	17 778.17	18 093.50	18 948.15
EEC (12)	18 324.38	19 093.74	19 534.17	19 800.97	20 630.14

Deflated using Gross Fixed Capital Formation Price Index.

Table 11. **Per capita investment by common carriers: 3-year moving average**
(US$ in 1980 prices & exchange rates)

	1975-77	1977-79	1979-81	1981-83	1983-85
Australia	76.08	79.23	187.54	310.87	75.16
Austria	62.79	61.30	64.25	73.12	83.01
Belgium	60.44	55.23	53.70	57.84	59.41
Canada	84.86	83.06	88.97	79.50	73.13
Denmark	66.71	67.43	62.71	53.99	53.52
Finland	69.32	61.12	55.68	59.19	62.86
France	85.42	104.87	96.36	83.86	82.54
Germany	58.48	65.13	82.72	91.74	103.57
Greece	20.75	19.70	24.86	33.03	32.80
Iceland	3 498.59	3 752.04	2 737.72	38.38*	49.34
Ireland	47.83	43.93	64.79	89.70	44.65
Italy	56.73	55.91	49.62	53.18	58.88
Japan	57.94	59.37	56.85	56.11	56.27
Luxembourg	55.42	64.46	42.01	25.85	30.77
Netherlands	49.06	49.57	44.23	37.36	39.93
New Zealand	0.00	7.24	17.71	23.86	38.45
Norway	85.35	105.33	104.74	98.92	98.17
Portugal	13.53	12.64	14.61	17.26	18.29
Spain	55.01	49.39	43.09	40.46	39.01
Sweden	37.11	36.03	59.87	93.67	93.15
Switzerland	112.89	103.88	99.63	108.81	117.48
Turkey	5.38	4.35	1.20	2.39	9.64
United Kingdom	52.80	44.39	48.77	50.34	49.42
United States	71.32	80.50	82.09	71.13	67.39
OECD	61.59	65.25	67.68	66.36	62.10
EEC(10)	60.58	63.78	65.68	66.52	69.45
EEC(12)	58.49	60.51	61.44	61.90	64.21

* Currency reform.

Table 12. **United States: telecommunications equipment**[1]

($ million)

	Value of shipments	Exports	Imports	Apparent consumption	Export ratio	Import ratio
1973	5 025	111.8	125.2	5 038	2.2	2.5
1974	5 880	160.0	162.3	5 882	2.7	2.8
1975	5 492	197.8	93.1	5 387	3.6	1.7
1976	5 890	226.5	93.7	5 757	3.8	1.6
1977	7 858	257.2	128.7	7 729	3.3	1.7
1978	8 834	388.2	232.9	8 679	4.4	2.7
1979	10 677	447.5	319.0	10 548	4.2	3.0
1980	12 283	557.0	420.6	12 147	4.5	3.5
1981	13 268	653.2	494.6	13 109	4.9	3.8
1982	13 394	829.0	626.0	13 191	6.2	4.7
1983	13 527	790.0	1 209.0	13 946	5.8	8.7
1984	15 783	777.0	1 817.0	16 823	4.9	10.8
1985	18 197[2]	832.0	2 028.0	19 393	4.6	10.4
1986	20 745[2]	850.0	2 185.0	22 080	4.1	9.9

Source: U.S. Industrial Outlook : 1985, 1987.
1. SIC 3661, data do not include microwave systems, mobile radio systems, data communications systems, and satellite communications systems.
2. Estimated.

Table 13. Japan: telecommunications equipment*
(Millions of U.S. dollars converted at current exchange rate)

	Production	Exports	Imports	Apparent consumption	Export ratio	Import ratio
1973	1 553.9	104.4	5.5	1 455.0	6.7	0.4
1974	1 505.1	125.5	9.7	1 389.3	8.3	0.7
1975	1 350.8	145.2	9.2	1 214.8	10.7	0.8
1976	1 324.4	188.6	10.9	1 146.7	14.2	1.0
1977	1 611.6	209.7	16.1	1 418.0	13.0	1.1
1978	2 393.5	354.2	17.9	2 057.2	14.8	0.9
1979	2 604.2	387.1	23.2	2 240.3	14.9	1.0
1980	2 655.1	395.6	21.4	2 280.9	14.9	0.9
1981	3 195.2	566.7	21.5	2 650.0	17.7	0.8
1982	3 217.6	790.1	25.9	2 539.4	24.6	1.0
1983	3 951.3	939.2	33.1	3 045.2	23.8	1.1
1984	4 867.3	1116.6	40.7	3 791.4	22.9	1.1
1985	5 558.7	1378.1	57.6	4 238.2	24.8	1.4
1986	7 945.9	1755.4	84.5	6 275.0	22.1	1.3

Source: Electronics Industry Association of Japan.
* Excludes Radio Broadcasting Equipment.

Breakdown of production of telecommunications equipment
(Percentages)

	1976	1982	1983	1984	1985	1986
Telephone sets	6.0	4.7	5.7	6.3	7.6	7.6
Switching systems	36.7	30.1	25.8	24.0	22.4	24.4
Telephone-applied equipment*	11.1	18.7	23.6	26.1	20.0	18.6
Telegraph/facsimile equipment	10.1	18.5	18.9	22.7	24.7	23.7
Carrier transmission equipment	23.5	21.4	20.0	20.9	25.3	25.7
Other	12.6	6.6	6.0	–	–	–
Total:	100.0	100.0	100.0	100.0	100.0	100.0

Source: EIAJ.
* Includes key telephone systems, automatic answering devices and interphones.

Table 14. France: telecommunications equipment*
(Millions of francs)

	Sales	Exports	Imports	Apparent consumption	Export ratio	Import ratio
1972	3 891	359	143	3 675	9.2	3.9
1973	4 900	500	190	4 590	10.2	4.1
1974	6 307	684	271	5 894	10.8	4.6
1975	7 744	898	243	7 089	11.6	3.4
1976	8 638	1 053	348	7 933	12.2	4.4
1977	10 056	998	350	9 408	9.9	3.7
1978	11 446	1 077	374	10 743	9.4	3.5
1979	11 746	1 197	510	11 059	10.2	4.6
1980	12 820	1 488	517	11 849	11.6	4.4
1981	15 036	1 834	544	13 746	12.2	3.9
1982	17 067	2 492	666	15 241	14.6	4.4
1983	19 768	3 725	771	16 814	18.8	4.6
1984	22 218	4 275	787	19 059	19.2	4.1
1985	23 013	4 470	890**	19 433**	19.4	4.6
Growth 1972-84	15.6%	22.1%	15.3%	14.7%	5.6%	0.4%

Source: Fédération des Industries Electriques et Electroniques.
* NAP 2911
** Estimates.

Table 15. Germany: telecommunications equipment
(Millions of Marks)

	Production	Exports	Imports	Apparent consumption	Export ratio	Import ratio
1970	2 769.5	686.0	95.3	2 178.8	24.8	4.4
1976	4 545.9	1 472.7	221.4	3 294.6	32.4	6.7
1977	5 004.3	1 276.4	242.5	3970.4	25.5	6.1
1978	5 329.3	1 397.5	237.3	4 169.1	26.2	5.7
1979	6 180.1	1 407.0	257.0	5 030.1	22.8	5.1
1980	7 304.8	1 602.2	262.9	5 965.5	21.9	4.4
1981	7 557.5	1 833.9	299.0	6 022.6	24.3	5.0
1982	7 018.2	1 914.2	277.3	5 381.3	27.3	5.2
1983	7 143.1	1 768.7	303.6	5 678.0	24.8	5.3
Growth 1970-83	7.6%	7.5%	9.3%	7.6%		

Production of telecommunications equipment : product distribution
(Percentages)

	1977	1978	1979	1980	1981	1982	1983
Telephone (switches & sets)	64.5	62.7	60.4	61.3	63.5	65.9	63.4
Telegraph	12.6	14.1	14.0	11.6	11.1	7.5	6.5
Transmission	12.1	11.9	14.3	16.2	14.8	16.2	19.1
Other	1.6	1.7	1.6	1.5	1.5	1.6	1.9
Telecommunications equipment parts	9.1	9.4	9.7	9.4	9.0	8.7	9.0

Source: DAFSA, Les télécommunications dans le monde, Paris 1984.

Table 16. a) **United Kingdom: telegraph and telephone apparatus and equipment**

(£ million)

	Sales[1]	Exports	Imports	Apparent consumption	Export ratio	Import ratio
1978	588	98	54	544	16.7	9.9
1979	690	111	61	640	16.1	9.5
1980	943	97	70	916	10.3	7.6
1981	1 128	131	96	1 093	11.6	8.8
1982	1 275	144	125	1 256	11.3	10.0
1983	1 418	157	200	1 461	11.1	13.7
1984	1 475	183	234	1 526	12.4	15.3
1985	1 668	242	317	1 743	14.5	18.2

Source: U.K. Department of Trade and Industry.
1. Total sales of principal products.

b) **Sweden**

(Million Kroner)

	Production	Exports	Imports	Apparent consumption	Export ratio	Import ratio
1975	3 518	2 400	155	1 273	68.2	12.2
1980	4 468	3 429	292	1 331	76.7	21.9
1982	6 442	4 892	390	1 940	75.9	20.1
1984	8 138	6 936	1 011	2 213	85.2	45.7

Source: Elektronikindustrin i Sverige, Statistics Sweden, October 1986.

Sweden's production composition

(Percentage Distribution)

	1977	1980	1982
Central exchange equipment	67.3	59.2	63.8
Telephone sets	6.7	10.8	8.6
Teleprinters	0.1	2.5	1.4
Transmission equipment	7.7	8.9	12.2
Other	1.8	2.4	2.5
Parts	16.4	16.2	11.5

Source: DAFSA, *op. cit.*

Table 17. **Employment in the telecommunications equipment sector**

	France	Canada	United States	United Kingdom
1970	41 989			
1971	48 707			
1972	55 989		134 400	
1973	62 770		140 300	
1974	69 319		144 700	
1975	70 762		118 500	
1976	72 147		105 200	
1977	74 540		124 400	
1978	72 047	37 895	130 600	
1979	67 599	39 326	145 000	
1980	60 940	43 343	152 700	
1981	55 257	46 330	147 400	58 600
1982	54 983	45 629	136 900	57 000
1983	53 018	44 578	128 000	55 100
1984	51 589	47 651	133 000	50 800
1985	50 000	45 776	130 000	47 100
1986			126 000	42 900 (P)

P = preliminary

Output per man

	France (based on sales)	Canada	United States
	FF	$C	$
1973	78 063		35 816
1974	90 985		40 636
1976	119 723		55 988
1978	158 868	40 427	67 641
1980	210 371	53 734	80 439
1982	310 405	66 953	97 838
1983	372 854	65 817	105 679
1984	430 673	71 561	114 834

Sources: France – Fédération des Industries Electriques and Electroniques.
  U.S. – U.S. Industrial Outlook 1985, 1987.
  Canada – Department of Regional Industrial Expansion. Canadian data include electronic components employment and output.
  U.K. – Department of Industry.

Table 18. Telecommunications equipment exports by country

($ thousands)

	1978	1979	1980	1981	1982	1983	1984	CAGR*
Australia	2 965	8 392	11 262	11 586	19 252	24 444	8 979	20.3
Austria	14 502	17 964	21 673	19 008	21 103	24 355	24 944	9.5
Belgium/Luxembourg	274 859	266 874	414 584	296 177	233 685	241 385	196 531	-5.4
Canada	111 370	199 448	257 299	300 887	389 586	471 959	650 592	34.2
Denmark	73 410	86 401	99 977	96 382	93 011	92 252	92 502	3.9
Finland	16 127	28 229	62 319	80 226	87 997	104 099	97 031	34.9
France	419 968	491 858	558 323	477 206	594 347	703 851	579 887	5.5
Germany	874 150	965 929	1 108 916	1 010 655	1 005 648	905 425	895 652	0.4
Greece	8 932	19 075	17 113	11 685	12 620	10 747	9 922	1.8
Iceland	0	0	0	0	0	0	0	–
Ireland	20 492	29 308	55 167	73 035	95 456	80 125	100 914	30.4
Italy	171 235	169 928	190 618	197 158	247 167	223 648	232 088	5.2
Japan	902 755	839 177	976 014	1 332 471	1 502 960	1 887 312	2 445 030	18.1
Netherlands	350 273	469 621	543 999	440 117	266 247	225 520	267 718	-4.3
New Zealand	261	2 513	3 883	5 454	6 559	6 068	7 525	75.1
Norway	42 727	52 736	72 820	71 406	65 797	64 637	64 113	7.1
Portugal	6 827	10 346	10 155	13 278	11 016	6 346	5 219	-4.3
Spain	40 971	64 909	90 699	67 929	57 627	39 841	33 089	-3.5
Sweden	673 011	800 921	844 201	801 670	826 765	806 158	882 155	4.6
Switzerland	54 013	89 970	79 148	83 475	79 040	100 622	76 140	5.9
Turkey	97	9	1	133	1	124	1 325	54.6
United Kingdom	404 092	486 226	518 475	605 303	534 303	574 722	583 654	6.3
United States	674 354	795 126	888 476	1 036 425	1 235 358	1 154 114	1 109 760	8.6
EEC (10)	2 597 411	2 985 220	3 507 172	3 207 718	3 082 484	3 057 675	2 958 868	2.2
OECD Total	5 137 391	5 894 960	6 825 122	7 031 666	7 385 545	7 747 754	8 364 770	

Source: OECD
* Compound average growth rate.

110

Table 19. **Trade balance: total telecommunications equipment**
($ thousands)

	1978	1979	1980	1981	1982	1983	1984
Australia	-58 812	-97 970	-118 071	-179 758	-201 178	-212 319	-248 573
Austria	-81 335	-71 600	-69 638	-68 458	-54 044	-51 174	-61 400
Belgium/Luxembourg	166 775	125 906	227 817	133 455	105 516	129 992	94 402
Canada	-101 434	-16 049	26 533	5 276	114 137	108 048	205 588
Denmark	-28 087	-16 938	-18 558	15 477	21 052	16 510	660
Finland	-25 941	-36 169	-13 920	2 045	-2 263	25 787	17 998
France	301 393	327 650	371 297	292 268	433 094	554 042	445 664
Germany	665 167	734 548	863 985	799 366	827 693	729 498	712 226
Greece	-47 691	-22 044	-51 826	-35 898	-27 808	-22 573	-27 350
Iceland	-4 139	-6 445	-4 082	-5 427	-5 916	-6 407	-6 927
Ireland	-18 327	-23 161	-22 754	-44 349	-13 910	-9 469	13 800
Italy	71 053	38 145	12 900	37 676	73 464	30 785	12 143
Japan	792 083	790 102	920 802	1 236 870	1 368 471	1 744 161	2 304 200
Netherlands	149 981	246 271	262 468	256 386	106 400	67 619	99 057
ew Zealand	-18 704	-19 822	-14 494	-19 235	-23 505	-60 781	-50 419
Norway	-52 219	-49 155	-32 368	-38 214	-40 073	-43 778	-54 051
Portugal	-6 661	-9 389	-13 859	-18 549	-25 314	-21 085	-15 887
Spain	12 851	34 254	-17 790	-33 842	-46 683	-36 619	-31 276
Sweden	607 308	724 247	735 088	695 775	716 475	685 628	699 526
Switzerland	43 025	72 859	61 595	66 607	60 041	80 859	52 708
Turkey	-22 173	-24 049	-23 223	-28 260	-42 664	-33 667	-109 767
United Kingdom	242 553	279 708	243 541	251 532	162 085	117 782	100 479
United States	90 230	229 576	213 707	177 007	270 219	-406 519	-1 334 875
EEC (10)	1 502 817	1 690 085	1 888 870	1 705 913	1 687 596	1 614 186	1 451 081
EEC (10) (net)	1 483 893	1 602 091	1 841 816	1 639 400	1 679 904	1 593 422	1 362 502
OECD Total	2 770 395	3 200 270	3 562 437	3 526 010	3 817 953	3 419.987	2 927 693

Source: OECD.

SUMMARY OF TRENDS
IN CHANGING TELECOMMUNICATIONS SERVICE REGULATIONS:

United States

1956: Department of Justice and AT&T *Consent Decree* – prohibited AT&T and Western Electric from manufacturing any products not used by Bell Telephone System in providing communications services. AT&T required to grant all patents (prior and future) at reasonable cost.

1956: *Hush-A-Phone Decision* – permitted attachment of a device, not provided by the telephone company, to the telephone instrument.

1959: *Above 890 mhz Decision* authorized large private users to set up their own microwave facilities and use frequencies above 890.

1968: *Carterfone Decision* provided authorisation to attach customer-provided equipment to the network.

1969-1973: *Specialised Common Carrier Decisions.* An application for microwave long-distance facilities by MCI approved in 1969. Specialised Common Carrier Decision approved new entry of such carriers to offer long distance data transmission, facsimile and voice services.

1971: *Computer Inquiry I:* Decision that most combinations of computer and communications are not common carriage and therefore not subject to Communications Act. Principle of separation of "competitive" activities from "monopoly" activities put forward.

1972: *Open Skies II:* Domestic satellite communications carriers could be set up.

1974: *First Order Registration* programme of the FCC established for terminal equipment which allowed registered equipment to be directly connected to telephone system (did not cover telephone sets, key sets, and PBX equipment).

1974: *Antitrust Case* by Department of Justice against AT&T to separate AT&T from Western Electric and to split AT&T Long Lines into competing companies. Case came to trial in 1980 and settlement out of court reached in 1982 (Consent Decree) which led to Modified Final Judgement.

1976: *Resale and Shared Use:* Tariff restrictions on resale and shared use of leased lines eliminated.

1977: *Second Order Registration* programme extended 1974 FCC decision to cover telephone sets, key sets and PBXs.

1980: *Computer Inquiry II:* The FCC decided that customer premises equipment should not be regulated and AT&T was allowed to sell such equipment through a fully separate subsidiary. Such subsidiaries also required for enhanced services.